April 6, 2009

My Dear Sister
Tricia!
I wish you joy
on your journey back
HOME!

Love and Light
Nancy

The School of the New Spirituality Guidebook Series
in
"Applications for Life" Study Kits
Titles based on the *Conversations with God* Series
by Neale Donald Walsch

What God Wants - Kristin Stewart
Happier than God - Linda Lee Ratto
Communion with God - Maggie Reigh, Christina Erls-Daniels
Tomorrow's God - Christina Semple
Home with God - Kimberly Darwin
CONVERSATIONS WITH GOD with Teens Guidebook - Jeanne Webster,
Emily Welch
Conversations with God, Book 2 - Anne-Marie Barbier
Conversations with God, Book 3 - Alissa Goefran
Conversations with God, Book 1 - Nancy Lee Ways
Friendship with God - Donna Corso
The New Revelations - Patricia Glenn, Erma Watson

Life is our curriculum, lived in Love, Joy and Wisdom !

Each contains activities revealing new ways to think about God and fresh
ways to think about education. Inspired and based upon the wildly popular
NY Times best selling *Conversations with God* books, they are playful life
guides with discoveries and personal enrichment that you can practice for
your own growth.

What then?

You may easily use any guidebook as a workshop plan into your community.
Learning, of course, is lifelong and adding your touch by teaching with the
multi-sensory experiences in these guidebooks will expand your own
development and those in your world. Play away and see what miracles you
make.

~Linda Lee Ratto, EdM
SNS Executive Director

There are many different names for the divine source of creation; God,
any other name you prefer and hold to be your truth. What you call
your creative force depends upon your religion or dogma and beliefs,
each is equally sacred. For the sake of continuity and consistency and
while trying not to offend any person or group, we will use the term
"God."

Conversations with God
- an uncommon dialogue -

A Guidebook

for
CONVERSATIONS WITH GOD Book 1

by
Nancy Lee Ways

Illustrations by Alisha M. Ways

The *New Spirituality* is a way of honoring our natural impulse toward the Divine without making others wrong for the way in which *they* are doing it."

~ *Neale Donald Walsch*

Guidebook and Activities
for Conversations with God, Book 1
by
Nancy Lee Ways

ISBN 978-0-9819438-0-0

**Library of Congress
Catalogue Information,
and
Search Engine Topics:**

1. Education, 2. Enrichment Education, 3. Heart based
Education, 4. Spiritual Education, 5. Self Esteem, 6. Character
Development, 7. Values Education

Professionally Edited by:
Helene Camp
and
Mary Lee and Ray Hammond

Published by
SNS Press-SNS, Inc.
Post Office Box 622
Tyrone, Georgia 30290
USA

Table of Contents

Conversations with God
– an uncommon dialogue –

Book 1 Guidebook

based on

Neale Donald Walsch's

Conversations with God
– an uncommon dialogue –

Book 1

Guidebook

By Nancy Lee Ways, Co-Director, SNS Atlanta

Illustrations by Alisha M. Ways

Writer's Personal Introduction

Why I Am Writing this Guidebook
~ The Story of my Journey back to God ~

The writing experience has allowed me to grow immeasurable. Thus, I am writing this guidebook to help You understand Who You Really Are as well. I have made such progress on this long and seemingly hard journey to self-realization, my God realization, and I know that each of us is making that journey all through our days on this Earth.

There once was a time when I was "lost," as in the familiar song. I had no idea who I was and lived my life thinking everything that was important was on the outside of me. I couldn't hear the voice of God inside calling…calling…calling me Home.

I was a beautiful woman, married to a wonderful husband, and I had given birth to two healthy, happy daughters. We lived in a spacious home and were very active in our community school and church. I had everything I needed. I spent a lot of time with my family and drove the girls back and forth to school and their year around swim practice. Life was very hectic to say the least! My life would have seemed perfect to anyone looking in from the outside. However, I was not happy. I was living my life *outside of me* and I didn't know who I was.

God was calling me, yet I wasn't paying attention in little ways I now realize and have included many in the activities in this book. Before, the only time I talked to God was when I was in church. I believed in God, but thought He was somewhere out in the cosmos where I couldn't reach him. If I needed something, I would pray earnestly for him to answer my prayers. However, I never listened for an answer from God because I didn't think that was possible.

Then one day, God came calling again. This time the knock was louder, in the form of a huge wake-up call. Through a personal tragedy, the thing that I treasured more than anything else was taken away from me, my outside appearance, my so-called beauty. I lost the one thing that I thought defined Who I Really Was – and as a result I didn't see me as a beautiful woman anymore. I had lost my identity. I felt that God had deserted me. At times, I would scream out "There is no God!" Then when I was at my lowest, an angel came and told me that God doesn't care what you look like on the outside. God only cares about what is on the inside and God always sees you as beautiful.

After this, I was compelled to take a look within and somehow I knew there had to be something important in there. I started with questions. If what was on the outside of 'the real me' wasn't me, Who was I? What was this vast undiscovered space that I felt inside? This was the true beginning of my journey home – my journey back to God.

So I started on a grand adventure in search of me that lasted for ten years. I began by consciously deciding to change the way I was living my life. I also studied metaphysics, took lots of classes, met many new people, and traveled to foreign countries in search of information about other lives I had lived, that would define me. Things I didn't notice before, such as the beautiful world I lived in, began to become important to me. I began to move to a place of unconditional love and forgiveness for everyone and everything. And the hidden part of God became known to me. I learned there was a feminine part of God as well as masculine. This was called the Goddess. I began listening to that small still voice inside of me. I constantly searched and searched high and low for me.

I was told by wise ones that everything I had learned over the last ten years would prepare me for what I would be doing in the future. I was so anxious to get out in the world and do something with my new knowledge. Then a wonderful opportunity was presented to me. I was introduced to The School of the New Spirituality and the *Conversations with God* books by Neale Donald Walsch. Soon I was teaching children about the principles in the book and later was asked to become a Co-Director of SNS Atlanta.

About a year later, I began writing the activities and discoveries in this guidebook. As I studied *Conversations with God, Book I* and immersed myself deeply into its content, I traveled the road to personal transformation. This was the current culmination of my journey back to me – back Home again to God.

Where did my journey take me? Who did I discover I AM? I am God! God was and is inside of me! What I was looking for was right here the whole time waiting for me to remember it. I wasn't "lost" anymore. This knowing didn't come with a host of heavenly angels welcoming me home and I certainly didn't look any different. It was subtle, yet meaningful to me. This knowing, this joy, came from deep down inside of me and I simply now know Who I Am!

It is an illusion, as the *CONVERSATIONS WITH GOD* material states, that I "need anything," though everything I have done lead me to my knowing now, of course. Yet I realized I didn't need ten years of studying every book I could find. The years of classes I took were not necessary to find out Who I Am. The most profound searching, for me, was traveling within and then subsequently to foreign countries. All my inner and outer travels melded together in amazing ways, – but nothing is necessary. I finally awoke from the dream and returned to my Spirit Home, completing this phase of my personal evolution. From the moment of personal tragedy, through writing this guidebook and training with colleagues – there has been deep shifts within. Today I look back and all of a sudden a smile appears on my face. It feels as if I *can hear the angels applauding and welcoming me Home. This is now my current state of being – what a joy!*

Dedications

I dedicate this book to my loving and always supportive husband George. To my daughters Alisha and Aimee who are passionately moving through their own personal journeys.

Also, to Linda Lee Ratto who introduced me to the Conversations with God Book Series and the School of the New Spirituality. Linda's enthusiasm and beautiful open heart immediately made me want to be a part of this amazing "cutting edge of the future school." Her tireless dedication to her sacred work is such an inspiration to me, and I consider Linda a wonderful friend as well as colleague. My becoming a part of the SNS team has brought me to a place of knowing Who I Am and that is truly a gift beyond measure.

And, I dedicate this book to my Co-Director, Christina Semple, who I have thoroughly enjoyed working with and has become not only a colleague, but will be a life-long friend. Christina's vibrant young energy and passionate heart along with her strong leadership skills will enable her to create any career path that she chooses as she steps out into the world.

In addition, I dedicate this book to all my friends, the beautiful souls who have been there to assist me, in any way, on my transformational journey.

And lastly, I dedicate this book to all of you out there who are in the midst of your journey or are just beginning your journey back home – back home again to God.

Book Summary

Suppose you could ask God the most puzzling questions about existence – questions about love and faith, life and death, good and evil.

Suppose God provided clear, understandable answers.

It happened to Neale Donald Walsch. It can happen to you.

You are about to have a conversation . . . .

~ Neale Donald Walsch on the cover of
Conversations with God
– an uncommon dialogue –

How to Use This Guidebook

Chapter Summary –
Easy way to see the essence of each chapter, chockfull of practical spirituality messages.

Quotes –
Neale's and other spiritual leaders, to show the universality of the messages

Key Points –
Given to super-summarize what is contained in each chapter; easy to use for those sharing this material with others

New Spirituality Principles –
These are core beliefs from Neale's books, all are listed in Resource Section of this guidebook

Learning Objectives –
It is always a good idea to know what you are up to as you experience the activities

Prep and Materials –
Main ingredients are to be treated as special for your personal discovery experiences in this book, especially:
  a) Journal for your guidebook experiences, reflections, answers
  b) "My Conversations with God" pages are to pull out inspiring words for you to refer to any time you wish
  c) Calendar for your personal appointment with YOU

Activities –
  – For explorations of self
  – Some are offered for groups, too, so you move your new spirituality from your inside out; Activity contents may be easily shared with family, youth, friends, and colleagues.

Further Study –
Taking the learning into a lifelong learning practices

Questionnaires –
Meant for your personal development, especially important through each chapter, to create a practice of self-reflection and lifelong learning

Guidebook Introduction

Conversations with God
– an uncommon dialogue –

"I will speak to you if you will listen.
I will come to you if you will invite Me.
I will show you then that I have always been there.
All ways."

Conversations with God, Book 1 p.58

In preparing to use this Guidebook, it is essential to understand that God IS talking to us ALL the time and, in order to hear Him/Her, we must LISTEN. But, how do we do that in this fast paced, hurry up and do everything world? In this day and time, there are so many voices calling you to activities, schedules and to be so busy that you forget the peace of the Heart. Most of us are running out the door to get to work, come home tired at the end of the day and get up and do it all over again the next day. Others are rushing to get the kids off to school and then afterwards on to those never ending extra curricular activities like baseball, swimming, piano lessons and the like. When do we have time to LISTEN to God? There doesn't seem to be time for Self, much less God.

You really don't have to spend an inordinate amount of time praying or meditating to God, as many spiritual leaders have done in the past. The only thing you need to do is listen for God's messages that are being sent to you every minute of every day and in every way possible.

God will talk directly to you while you are right in the middle of living your life, when you least expect it and you never need any intermediaries. The keys to hearing this communication from God are Awareness and Going Within. These are principles that are explained in *Conversations with God* by the author, Neale Donald Walsch. Becoming aware of everything going on inside of you and around you is how you will notice when God is talking to you (within and without) and tuning in to that can completely change your life.

You will begin to move through your life consciously, instead of sleep walking through it as you may be now. By doing this, you will be taking care of Self better than you ever have been before and you will find you are having that conversation with God.

"He who lives in harmony with himself, lives in harmony with the universe."
Marcus Aurelius

"How much longer will you go on letting your energy sleep?

How much longer are you going to stay oblivious of the immensity of

yourself?

Don't lose time in conflict;

Lose no time in doubt – time can never be recovered and if you miss an

opportunity it may take many lives before another comes your way again."

Bhagwan Shree Rajineesh
A Cup of Tea

Creating Sacred Space to Communicate with God

A very special place to communicate with God can be made by creating a sacred space for YOU. This will allow you to have a secluded place to talk to God – a place to talk to God like you are talking to your best friend, one who cares about you and loves you. And God *does Love You just like that,* and unconditionally always.

Here, you will be able to more easily hear your inner voice that has been trying for so long to *get you to listen.* You might also enter into an altered state of consciousness. This special space will be a magical place where the physical and spiritual come together.

Now, let's create that sacred space! Think of a favorite place located in a separate room or just a special place set aside in a room in your home. Most importantly, it must be a quiet space where you can leave the noisy outside world behind. This will be your comfort place. You may sit in a chair or maybe on a special rug on the floor. This can also be a quiet place outside in nature, too, if you like.

"Begin by being still. Quiet the outer world, so that the inner world might bring you sight. This in-sight is what you seek, yet you cannot have it while you are so deeply concerned with your outer reality."

Conversations with God, Book 1, p.44

Perhaps you may like to set up an altar that holds objects that have a special meaning for you. You can cover a small table with a special cloth if you wish and then place your objects on top. Honoring the directions and the elements representing each is very powerful. I have included a description of these on the following page. You should do anything that creates a peaceful atmosphere for you including using lighted candles, crystals and incense.

Go to your special place at least once a day for about 30 minutes to communicate with God. Begin by sitting comfortably and inhaling deeply through your nose and imagine you are bringing Golden White Light from above the top of your head down through your channel to the base of your spine. You will be drinking in the elixir of Light that you truly are. Exhale slowly through your mouth and let all of the stresses of the day leave your body. As you inhale, again see the beautiful white pillar of light above your head and bring that all the way down to the base of your spine and connect this with the heart of dear Mother Earth.

Now exhale and send the light upwards to your crown and then inhale the light down again and hold your breath for a few seconds. This will ground you to Mother Earth and connect you to the Heavens. You will begin to feel completely relaxed and moving into a deeper meditative state of consciousness. Let the mind clutter quiet down, and eventually you will hear nothing but your own breathing. You will come to that place of stillness and connect with that peace that you are, that pure awareness. Now you are ready to have that conversation with God!

These guidebook activities are designed to open up a whole new world, revealing your vast inner terrain to you. I trust this guided journey will serve as a way to finding your true purpose in this wonderful thing called Life. Isn't that what life is all about – your journey to Self – your journey back to God and Oneness.

Background Information to Start this Guidebook Journey

Acknowledging and Honoring the Sacred Directions

Direction	Element	Sign	Archetype
North	Earth	Capricorn	Wise Elder
South	Water	Cancer	Great Mother
East	Fire	Aries	Warrioress Amazon
West	Air	Libra	Equal Partnership
Center	Spirit	As above so, below mysteries As within so, without mysteries	Sacred Divine Couple

At the end of your time in your sacred space, be sure to thank the Directions and Elements and release them.

Further Study:

Understand more about the messages of the elements, Earth, Water, Air, Fire, and Spirit by reading, Lisa Michaels' book, *Natural Rhythms.*

Learn more about the Sacred Directions and the Elements by reading *Nature Speak* by Ted Andrews

The Rays of Light

The Golden White Light is a combination of all the rays and connects you with God, Source or the Great Central Sun and divides into the Spectrum of Rainbow Colors

Blue	Divine Will, Power and Truth
Yellow	Enlightenment, Wisdom and Illumination
Pink	Transformational Love, Acceptance and Respect for all Life
Pure White	Purity, Hope, Clarity and Ascension
Emerald Green	Alignment, Balance and Harmony
Ruby Red/Gold	Grace, Devotion and Peace
Violet	Freedom, Compassion, Forgiveness and Transmutation

The violet light is the highest frequency you can see with the naked eye. Surround yourself, and any condition in your life that is discordant, daily with this frequency. You will transform the condition into one of harmony and peace.

The pink light is the color of self-love and resonates with the soul. Send this frequency out to others and to the universe and the world will be a much happier place.

You are a Great Ray of Light!

"The feeling of attraction and the intense and often urgent desire to move toward each other, to become one, is the essential dynamic of all that lives."

Conversations with God, Book 1, p. 207

The Creation Mysteries of the Universe

The Yin or feminine (negative) and the Yang or masculine (positive) energies are essential in all creative processes. I am not speaking of the gender difference between men and women. What I refer to is the masculine and feminine energies that exist in every one of us, including God. Remember, you are made in the image of God. These energies are not only found in the physical, they exist in the mental and spiritual planes as well. They comprise every sub particle of the universe and are the foundation of creation itself. Yin and Yang represent the type of effort that is needed for all creativity.

The masculine is recognized by scientists as being a part of the left brain and ideal for analytical functions and initiating action. The feminine demonstrates more right brain activity and is designed for creativity and intuitive functions. Both of these principles must be there to manifest anything in our three dimensional world. A part of balanced and healthy spiritual development is to understand and express both the masculine and feminine energies. Allow them to be and without judgment of one as better than the other; they are equivalent in their differences!

According to the book, *The Light Shall Set You Free, "the receptive side of humanity's nature is often called the negative side. This is further termed the feminine or yin. This is the force that creates, spins ideas, and weaves the threads to make the tapestry into a work of art."*

"The positive or directive side of humanity's nature is called the masculine or yang. This force is directed toward the creative force of the feminine principle. It is the originator of ideas and actions. The masculine energy is attracted to the feminine principle and when they unite, they form a union that assures that the creative process will be realized."

The Light Shall Set You Free
Dr. Norma Milanovich and Dr. Shirley McCune
p. 243, 244

All consciousness contains these two mysteries of the universe and when there is a balance in both of the principles within the soul, you will know how and when to act in all situations. On our planet, the feminine principle has been suppressed for centuries. The masculine principle has been dominant, making it nearly impossible for men and women to realize their full human potential.

As a result of this aggressive principle, there has been a period of never ending wars, a lack of socio economic equality and destruction at every turn. Now, after such a long period of time, balance of the feminine principle is being restored by God on our planet. The Goddess energy is returning. This will bring about the balance needed within each of us to become a co-creator with God. As this occurs, you will have full knowledge of Self.

Further Study:

To understand more about the return of the balance of the divine feminine, you may want to study the planetary alignment called the Venus Transit.

Conversations with God
– an uncommon dialogue –

Chapter 1

Summary

The most important message in this chapter, and in fact the entire book, is that God is willing and does communicate with EVERYONE ALL THE TIME. HE/SHE sends these messages through feelings, thoughts, experience and sometimes words that can often be misunderstood. God tells the book's author, Neale Donald Walsch, that these messages have been sent for eons of time, and you are not receiving them because you have stopped listening. You are not aware that they are being sent out. God loves you unconditionally and says that He/She will continue to send those same messages until you do LISTEN.

God is the observer of humanity and has always given you free choice to create yourself and your reality and experience it in any way you choose, including your decision to live in separation from God. However, in truth, you are God. You are a divine part of the whole. You are not separate.

"My purpose for creating you, My spiritual offspring, was for Me to know Myself as God. I have no way to do that save through you. Thus, it can be said (and has been, many times) that My purpose for you is that you should know yourself as Me."

Conversations with God, Book 1, p.26

Therefore, every moment in your life is an opportunity to come to a place of Self-Realization of Who You Really Are. Who are you? You are LOVE. And that is the message that God has been trying to get you to hear for so long.

"From the highest mountain it has been shouted, in the lowest place its whisper has been heard. Through the corridors of all human experience has this Truth been echoed: Love is the answer. Yet you have not listened."

Conversations with God, Book 1, p. 58

"The body is the temple of God; in every body, God is installed whether the owner of the body recognizes it or not. It is God that inspires you to good acts, that warns you against the bad. Listen to that voice. Obey that voice, and you will not come to any harm."

Sathya Sai Baba
The Lightworker's Way, p.43
DoreenVirtue, Ph.D

"What lies before us and what lies behind us are small matters compared to what lies within us. And when we bring what is within out into the world, miracles happen."

Henry David Thoreau
Karen Bishop
Remembering Your Soul Purpose, p. xvii

Chapter 1 Key Points

- God communicates with everyone all the time

- Feeling is the language of the soul

- The tools of creation are thought, word and deed

- All Sponsoring thoughts of either Love or Fear

- You learn Who You Are Not in order to know Who You *Really Are*

- If I do not go within, I go without

- There is no right and wrong

- Love is the only answer

- Why you bring what you fear to you

New Spirituality Principles

- ❖ God has never stopped communicating directly with human beings. God has been communicating with and through human being from the beginning of time. God does so today.

- ❖ You and God are one. There is no separation between you. From: Sixth of 18 Remembrances (from *Home with God*)

- ❖ Four Holistic Living Principles:
  - Awareness
  - Responsibility
  - Honesty
  - Gratitude

> *"Go ahead now. Ask me anything. Anything. I will contrive to bring you the answer. The whole universe will I use to do this. So be on the lookout. This book is far from My only tool. You may ask a question, then put this book down. But watch, Listen. The words to the next song you hear. The information in the next article you read. The story line of the next movie you watch. The chance utterance of the next person you meet. The whisper of the next river, the next ocean, the next breeze that caresses your ear – all these devices are Mine; all these avenues are open to Me. I will speak to you if you will listen. I will come to you if you will invite Me. I will show you then that I have always been there. All ways."*
>
> ~ *Neale Donald Walsch*
> *Conversations with God, Book 1, p. 58*

Objectives

- To learn that God does communicate with you.
- To experience how to be aware of your environment and "tune in" to receive God's messages.
- To invite God to come into your life.
- To notice and record what is happening in the world around you, within and without.
- To become aware of feelings, thoughts, experiences and sometimes words that seem to draw you inside; these are portals that can open up a whole new world for you.
- To understand what God is trying to tell you, feel a closer connection with God and be able to move forward with more purpose in your life and happiness in your soul.

Preparation and Materials

- Set aside a time period of 30-60 minutes several times a week for these activities and continue your observation of the messages God sends you for at least three weeks.
- You will need a notebook or journal and a pen or pencil.

Activity A

Now is the time to take notice of all of the messages that God is sending you and record them in a journal or notebook. Also, be sure to answer the questions in this activity and write those in your notebook. The first part of this exercise is for you to consciously invite God to send you the answers to your prayers or questions. This can be done in your sacred space or anywhere you wish. Next, be sure you thank God for those answers and open yourself with intention to receive them. Gratitude is the key. Does it seem strange to you to thank God before even asking the question?

"When you thank God in advance for that which you choose to experience in your reality, you, in effect, acknowledge that it is there...in effect. Thankfulness is thus the most powerful statement to God; an affirmation that even before you ask, I have answered."

Conversations with God, Book 1, p.11

Can you talk to God like you are having a conversation with a good friend? Does that feel comfortable to you? Remember, God does not want your worship. God wants you to communicate.

Now, write down in your book anything that catches your attention, any feelings you may have, thoughts, experiences, words that seem to keep coming to you over and over again or pictures that appear in your mind.

In your notebook, divide the communication into the category of Feelings, Thoughts, Words, and Experiences. Each time you receive a message, put that in the proper category. You will begin to notice what is calling for your attention, such as a scene in a movie, a picture in a magazine, a bird outside on your patio. You may see a message in a word or words on a sign outside, or a book that is asking you to pick it up. There can be a message anywhere. Be aware of everything around you. When God wants to talk to you, He/She will send you a message that only you will notice. You should take note of everything and contemplate what the meaning may be.

Date	Feelings	Thoughts	Words	Experiences

The answers to your questions may not come immediately. However, by staying tuned in to life, you will see, know, feeling, sense answers custom-made for you. Are you becoming aware of things you never noticed before? What way are you receiving the most communication? Why do you think you didn't notice these things before? Are you feeling a little more sensitive to the environment now? Do you want to tell everyone that they should pay attention, too?

Activity B

1. You can hear many messages from God through nature. Take the time to go outside, perhaps on a ten minute walk through your neighborhood. Or this can be done on your lunch break at work.

2. Animals, birds and flowers can bring us messages from God and help us learn more about ourselves. Most already know that a robin means springtime and spread of new growth. It also "reflects a need to sing your own song forth if you wish new growth", as stated in the comprehensive dictionary of animal, bird and reptile symbolism resource book "Animal Speak" by Ted Andrews.

3. Pay attention to everything you feel and see and keep a record each day for the next week of how God is communicating with you through nature. I suggest you find a copy of the above book and also "Nature Speak" by the same author, which contains the meaning of signs, omens and messages in nature. There are many similar books on the market that you could use as well, in addition to information on the internet. Some of them may be available in your local library, too.

4. When you take time to pay attention to the spiritual and magical powers of an animal, it reflects to you lessons that are necessary for you to learn in order to navigate through life. Here are a few messages from birds and animals to get you started:

Bird	Message
Cardinal	Renewed vitality through recognizing self-importance
Ducks	Emotional comfort and protection
Finch	Energy of variety & multiplicity (everything in your life will amplify)
Red Tailed Hawk	Visionary power and guardianship (tied to kundalini)
Woodpecker	The power of rhythm and discrimination (safe to follow your own rhythms)

Animal	Message
Armadillo	Personal protection, discrimination, and empathy
Bear	Awakening the power of the unconscious
Cougar	Coming into your own power
Groundhog	Mystery of death without dying – trance – dreams
Panther	Reclaiming one's true power (imminent rebirth)

Reference: *Animal Speak* by Ted Andrews; *Nature Speak* by Ted Andrews

Group Activity

Get together with other people and have fun talking about how they receive communication from God. You can begin each meeting by having everyone contribute to a sacred space and then talk about what has been going on in their lives. Each person should have a chance to contribute if she/he wishes. This can be a way of bringing people together and sharing information.

Chapter 1 Questions

Write the answers to these questions in your notebook. There is no right or wrong answer. This is for your reflection on what you have learned in the chapter.

Do you believe that God is and has always been with you?

What was your relationship with God like when you were a child? Did you ever talk to God then? Did you hear God talking back to you?

Did you ever communicate with the animals around you?

Who is God?

Was there a particular time in your past when you felt God working through you to help other people?

What does surrendering to God mean to you?

Do you always make decisions based on feelings of love?

Who have you decided you are not?

What does "Love is the only answer" mean to you?

Further study:

Begin a study of the animal kingdom and discover what message each animal wants to share with you.

Study the magical nature kingdom and learn what messages the flowers, trees and plants have for you.

Questionnaire

Write the answers in your notebook. These questions are to assist you in recognizing your personal growth after reading this chapter.

What have you learned about yourself after doing these activities?

What feelings did you have during the chapter activities?

Did you change in any way after reading this chapter and doing the activities? If yes, how?

How have you changed in the way you relate to others after reading this chapter and doing the activities?

Conversations with God
– an uncommon dialogue –

Chapter 2

Summary

Who is this God who loves you and wants you to communicate with Him and how do you come to this place of Self-Realization? Chapter two explains God is both masculine and feminine (as explained in the Divine Creation Mysteries at the front of this book) and is found everywhere. There is a part of God in every one of us, and we need not look outside of us for Her. God is in the oceans, the streams, the grass we walk on in our backyards, in happy times and times of sadness, in loving feelings and is even found in what we call "evil". God has a divine purpose behind everything and there is a divine presence in everything. Therefore, by experiencing evil, we can understand good. We have to learn what We Are Not before we can know Who We Are. There is nothing that is not a part of God.

"Everything is "acceptable" in the sight of God, for how can God not accept that which is? To reject a thing is to deny that it exists. To say that it is not okay is to say that it is not a part of Me – and that is impossible."

Conversations with God, Book 1, p. 61

The author explains that God does not have any needs, only desires.

God says to the author, *"I desire first to know and experience Myself, in all my glory – to know Who I Am. Second, I desire that you shall know and experience Who You Really Are, through the power I have given you to create and experience yourself in whatever way you choose. Third, I desire for the whole life process to be an experience of constant joy, continuous creation, never-ending expansion, and total fulfillment in each moment of now."*

Conversations with God, Book 1, p. 65

Your Self-Realization is accomplished by everything you experience. This is how you know Who You Truly Are. However, God tells us that most of us have determined Who We Are based upon the experiences of others. He says this is our greatest sin (if there were such a thing as sin). Therefore, in this journey to Self-Realization, it is necessary to examine your belief system and decide if this serves you based on Who You Want to Be. Are you happy with your beliefs? Do they serve you? Or are they based on people such as your parents, teachers historians or religious leaders?

"People get caught in the trap of the mind and become lazy when it comes to changing attitudes and beliefs about life. Change requires effort. And to change beliefs about yourself and the world around you necessitates focusing your thoughts consistently on your goal or objective. It means being open to different ways of thinking and attitudes and releasing old patterns that no longer serve you. It means giving yourself the freedom to pick and choose the beliefs that will add the most value to your life. When you live with the flexibility of choosing your beliefs, you can indeed change your life."

The Soul Never Sleeps
Marian Masse, p.35

Chapter 2 Key Points

- God is both masculine and feminine

- There is a divine presence in everything

- Everything is acceptable to God

- God needs nothing and requires nothing from us

Five Attitudes of God

Do your beliefs serve you?

You are worthy to be spoken to by God

New Spirituality Principles

- ❖ Awareness
- ❖ Responsibility
- ❖ Honesty
- ❖ Gratitude

- ❖ Main questions to ask when creating New Spirituality Beliefs:

- ❖ What works and what does not work?
  - o Is my belief FUNCTIONAL?
  - o Is my belief ADAPTABLE?
  - o Is my belief SUSTAINABLE?

- ❖ Tomorrow's God is without gender, size, color, or any of the characteristics of an individual living being.

- ❖ God needs nothing. God requires nothing in order to be happy. God is happiness itself. Therefore, God requires nothing of anyone or anything in the Universe.

"Yet hold to your beliefs, and stay true to your values, for these are the values of your parents, of your parents' parents; of your friends and of your society. They form the structure of your life, and to lose them would be to unravel the fabric of your experience. Still, examine them one by one. Review them piece by piece. Do not dismantle the house, but look at each brick, and replace those which appear broken, which no longer support the structure."

~ Neale Donald Walsch
Conversations with God, Book 1, p. 61

Objectives

- To understand, through an examination of your current beliefs, what beliefs are the basis of your current vision of Who You Really Are.

- To also learn the concept of releasing the old (which is based on what others have told you or what no longer serves you) to make room for the new.

Preparation and materials

- You will need 3 small boxes (about shoe box size), scissors and paper, pen or pencil.
- Cut the paper into approximately 30 strips and label one box My Current Beliefs, the second, Other People's Beliefs, and the third My New Beliefs.

Activity C

1. Begin this exercise by writing down one of your current beliefs on each piece of paper about such things as God, self, your parents, teachers, friends, religion, things you align yourself with politically, economically, beliefs about your health and any others you can think of. Place these "belief strips" in the first box, My Current Beliefs. You may need additional strips of paper.

2. Next, place the other strips of paper in the third box, labeled My New Beliefs. Think about the beliefs you wrote down. Are they based on your experience or that of others? After some deep reflection on this question, ask yourself (1) Is my belief functional? (2) Is my belief adaptable? (3) Is my belief sustainable? Is it my own? Put those beliefs in the first box.

3. The next day, take any beliefs that are based on anything other than your own experience, and if they no longer serve you, place them in the Other People's Beliefs Box. Put the others that continue to serve you back in the first box.

4. Take time now to reflect on what you now believe about these things. You may be shocked to see that many of the things you took as "truth" came from what someone told you or another source of information.

5. Do you have the courage to render your original teacher or source as wrong? Maybe not wrong, because *Conversations with God* tells us that there is no *"right or wrong."* However, if you listen to your heart (not your mind) to answer this question, what do you believe now?

6. Take the strips of paper out of the third box and write down your "new beliefs" regarding each thought. Put these in the third box.

7. Next, it is important to release the beliefs that no longer serve you that you placed in the second box. This can be done only with intention, or you can create a little ceremony to accomplish this. You may want to go outside and place each of the "old belief" strips in a bowl and then, as you say out loud what you are releasing, light the strips of paper with a white candle. After they have burned, scatter the ashes and let the wind carry them away from you.

Alternate Activity

Make a "Release Doll" or "Release Ball". Look around your house for something which represents those "Old Beliefs". These may be such things as old pictures, or sketches you create yourself, anything you have around your home, or you may want to make a list of the "old beliefs" Next fashion these items into a doll or ball, securing with string, if necessary. Then follow the ceremony for releasing that is above. How do you feel after releasing these things?

Activity D

How do you picture God? Draw a picture of what you believe God looks like. This is a creative process just for you, based on your image of God and no one else's. *Conversations with God* tells you that you are made in the image of God. Now draw a picture of yourself. Enjoy the process of Self-realization.

"If you think God looks only one way or sounds only one way or is only one way, you're going to look right past Me night and day. You'll spend your whole life looking for God and not finding Her. Because you're looking for a Him."

~ Neale Donald Walsch
Conversations with God, Book 1, p. 60

Preparation and Materials

- You will need approximately 30 minutes during your day to complete this next activity and your notebook to write in.
- Reread the "Creation Mysteries of the Universe" at the front of this Guidebook. Think about the characteristics of masculine and feminine essence that everyone carries inside of them.

Activity E

Conversations with God explains that God is both masculine and feminine. You have that same essence in you. In your notebook write Masculine on one side of the paper and Feminine on the other. Make a list of how you express your masculine essence and feminine essence. Remember these are generalities and you may well find you have always been a blend of both energies.

Masculine	Feminine
Resistant to change	Open to all things
Controlling	Detached
Add more…	Add more…

Does one side of your paper include more than the other?
In order for you to co-create with God, can you strive to find balance in each? How do you think you can accomplish that? List those in your notebook.

Questions for further reflection: Write the answers in your notebook.

Can you forgive others for passing on their beliefs to you?

Are you capable of forgiving yourself for taking these beliefs on as your own?

If God wants nothing from you, why are you working so hard to please Him/Her?

When you are communicating with God in your sacred place or any other place, for that matter, what type of person do you think God wants you to be?

Don't forget about your boxes! From time to time, when you notice that a belief of yours no longer serves you, take that out of the first box and place in the second box, Other People's Beliefs, and when you create a new belief, place that in the appropriate "New Beliefs" box. After a time, you may not need your three Belief Boxes anymore. You will think consciously and with your heart before taking on someone else's beliefs as your own.

Chapter 2 Questions

Write the answers to these questions in your notebook. There is no right or wrong answers. This is for your reflection on what you have learned in the chapter.

There are wars being fought in many places in our world. Can you see God's divine presence in that?

Do you feel it is necessary to worship God?

What does God want from you?

Do you believe that you are worthy to be spoken to by God?

Is there anyone who you believe is not worthy to be spoken to by God?

Further Study:

Read more about the Divine Masculine and Divine Feminine Energies

Think about the inequalities of masculine and feminine energies in the world of ages past and our current time. Chart, scribe or otherwise document about your feelings, and then think about, and list ways you believe more of a balance can be brought about in the future.

	Past Event or Belief	Current Event or Belief
Feminine		
Masculine		

To learn more about the feminine or Goddess energy, read, *The Book of the Goddess Past and Present* by Carl Olson or *Mary Magdalene and the Divine Feminine*, a book by Elizabeth Clare Prophet

Questionnaire

Write the answers in your notebook. These questions are to assist you in recognizing your personal growth after reading this chapter.

What did you learn about yourself after these activities?

What feelings did you have during the chapter activities?

Did you change in any way after reading Chapter 2 and doing the activities
If yes, How?

How have you changed in the way you relate to others after reading this chapter?

Conversations with God
– an uncommon dialogue –

Chapter 3

Summary

God has established laws in the universe, in partnership with you (a holy collaboration) to make it possible for you to create anything you choose. In that journey of creation, you agreed to forget and veil yourself from the memory that you are a son or daughter of God and made of the same essence.

"You are his son. Her offspring. Its likeness. His equal."
Conversations with God, Book 1, p.75

This is God's promise to you. God tells the author that His Grandest Wish-Grandest Desire for you is to experience yourself as the God or Goddess that you are. You are a child of God. You are not your body, as has been assumed for eons by humanity. Your God essence is made up of three parts: body, mind and spirit. The mind and body are servants of the soul. You were given the tools of creation; thought, word and deed (or action) in order that you may re-create or re-member Who You Really Are. The soul guides you through this process and wants to experience everything, THE ALL THAT IS, in order to evolve. Great frustration and anxiety occurs in our life as a result of not listening to our soul. Do you realize that your soul is trying to get your attention and are you listening?

"The highest feeling is the experience of unity with All That Is. This is the great return to Truth for which the soul yearns. This is the feeling of perfect love."
Conversations with God, Book 1, p. 83

"Simply stated, you are Soul. You are not a body with a soul, you ARE Soul. Soul is a happy, joyful, loving entity. For now, realize that you are Soul and, as Soul, you are an individualized and unique expression of God. We are all part of God."

Marian Massie
Soul Never Sleeps, p. 55

"In order to develop and nurture your mind and your body, it is necessary to realize that you have a mind and body. To heal directly at the level of the soul it is first necessary to acknowledge that you have a soul. If you have a soul, is it hollowness that mythologically fills your ribcage? No. If, then, your soul is real and alive with force and beingness, what is its purpose?"

Gary Zukav
The Seat of the Soul, p. 194

Chapter 3 Key Points:

- God has given us Universal laws
- You consist of body, mind and spirit (The Holy Trinity)
- The tools of creation are thought, word and deed
- You are a part of God and God's equal
- Call forth your highest vision of self
- All conditions are temporary
- You are not your body
- Your soul wants you to evolve

New Spirituality Principles

❖ You are not your body. Who you are is limitless and without end.

❖ Three Core Concepts of Holistic Living:

1. Awareness

2. Honesty

3. Responsibility

❖ Truth-telling

1. Tell the Truth to yourself about yourself.

2. Tell the Truth about yourself to another.

3. Tell the Truth about another to that other.

❖ Choose to live your life as a demonstration of your highest and grandest beliefs, rather than as denials of them.

"Now having seen the differences between where you are and where you want to be, begin to change – consciously change – your thoughts, words, and actions to match your grandest vision."

~ Neale Donald Walsch
Conversations with God, Book 1, p.77

"Think, speak, and act as the God that You Are."

~ Neale Donald Walsch
Conversations with God, Book 1, p. 76

Objectives

▪ To move you to a higher consciousness vs. unconsciousness

▪ To call forth your Highest "Truth" or "Vision" of everything in your life.

▪ To reveal and unveil great happiness when you find yourself in your God space ready to listen to what your soul truly wants.

Preparation and Materials

You will need:
- your notebook
- a foam core board approximately the size of a half piece of poster board
- a sheet of letter size paper
- pens, crayons, paints, glue and anything for decorating.

Activity F

1. In your notebook, list the following areas of your life and write down what your current thoughts are about them (You may add some others if you wish):

Topic	Current Belief	Highest Vision
God		
Self		
Religion		
Family		
Friends		
Pets		
Work		
Money		
Community		
Local Governance		
National Government		
Our Planet		
The Cosmos.		
Other topic		
other topic		

2. Now, think about what your "Highest Vision" for each of these things in your life would be, and write them in your notebook next to what you currently think. Here are some examples of questions you can ask yourself while doing this part of the activity:

a) Do you believe that God is a loving God? What is your highest thought about God?

b) What about yourself? What is your highest thought about you? Do you believe you are made in the image of God? How healthy is your body? Are you happy?

c) What about your religion? Does it serve you? What is the highest thought you can think of regarding that?

d) What about your family? Do you love them unconditionally? What is your highest thought about them?

3. Continue to write down your highest thought for each part of your life. When you are happy with your highest thoughts in each area of your life, write these down on a new sheet of paper and title it "My Highest Visions." You could use attractive script and decorate this any way you want. Then glue these "Highest Visions" on the piece of foam core board and decorate that if you wish. Or you can frame this and place it on the wall.

4. Place this in your sacred space or anywhere you can see it every day. Begin to think, speak and act these "Highest Visions" every moment of every day.

Objective

- To become aware of the energy or spiritual body

Preparation and materials and reading activity

- Please read the following background information giving you a clearer description of how the energy bodies work and their relationship with the physical body before doing the next activities.

- In addition to the physical body that you use to experience life, there is another body, which is vital for daily creation and spiritual growth. This is your energy body or spiritual body, which Neale Donald Walsch talks about in Chapter 3. This energy system exists in other dimensions, and is invisible to the human eye. One of these unseen worlds or systems of energy was defined thousands of years go by Hermes and was called the chakra system. During ancient times, most people did not believe in something that they could not see, and this knowledge was lost for a period of time. In today's world, modern technology such as the electro-encephalogram (EEG) and the electrocardiogram (EKG) and the super conductive interference device (SQUID) can measure these energy fields, therefore, scientists now know they really do exist. These seven energy centers are like spinning wheels (chakra is wheel in Sanskrit), and are contained in our auric field. They correspond to the colors of the rainbow. Each of these energy centers correlates to one of the areas of your physical body and extends out from the body in your egg shaped magnetic field.

– There are four of these multidimensional energy systems. Barbara Ann Brennan, a scientist-healer with psychic sight, describes these four dimensions of energy systems and their inter-relationships. These are listed below:

Energy or Spiritual Bodies

➤ The Physical Body – the body that behaves in relationship to the other dimensions

➤ The Aura, including the chakras – the personality that we develop

➤ The Hara – the foundation for the personality which is created out of our intentions

➤ The Core Star Level – our divine essence

There are Seven Levels to the Aura.

Please see diagram (a). They are:

Level 1   Physical   *Etheric*

Level 2   Emotional

Level 3   Mental

Level 4   Astral (Relationships and

             Compassion)

Level 5   Etheric (Divine Will)   *Body*

Level 6   Celestial (Soul)   *Rain Bow*

Level 7   Ketheric or Causal (Divine

         Mind)   *Diamond Body*

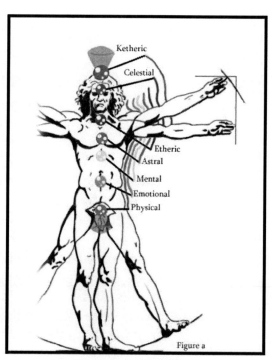

Figure a

Illustration by Alisha Ways

The Light Shall Set You Free
Dr. Norma Milanovich
Dr. Shirley McCune, p. 71

The seven chakras are openings for the energy to flow into and out of the aura.
See Diagram (b)

Chakra	Where Located	Color
First or Root Chakra	Base of spine	Red
Second or Sacral Chakra	Below naval	Orange
Third or Solar Plexus Chakra	Solar plexus	Yellow
Fourth or Heart Chakra	Heart center	Green
Fifth or Throat Chakra	Throat	Blue
Sixth or Third Eye Chakra	Brow	Indigo Blue
Seventh or Crown	Top of head	Violet

Illustration by Alisha Ways

Figure b

Each Chakra governs an area of the body, a gland and a specific psychological function.

Chakra	Corresponding Area of Body	Gland
First	Spinal column, Kidneys	Adrenals
Second	Reproductive system	Gonads
Third	Stomach, Liver, Gall bladder, Nervous system	Pancreas
Fourth	Heart, Blood, Vagus nerve, Circulatory system	Thymus
Fifth	Bronchial and vocal apparatus, Lungs	Thyroid
Sixth	Lower brain, Left eye, Ears, Nose, Nervous system	Pituitary
Seventh	Upper brain, Right eye	Pineal

Chakras and the Psychological Issues

First	Survival	Grounding, prosperity, physical
Second	Sexuality, emotions	Pleasure
Third	Power, energy	Strength of will, purpose
Fourth	Love	Balance, compassion
Fifth	Communication	Clear communication, creativity
Sixth	Intuition	Psychic perception, imagination
Seventh	Understanding	Wisdom, spiritual connection

> *"You are a three-fold being. You consist of body, mind and spirit. You could also call these the physical, non-physical, and the meta-physical."*
>
> ~ Neale Donald Walsch
> *Conversations with God, Book 1*, p. 73

Objectives

- To feel your energy or spiritual body and how it interacts with others through various activities.

You have felt the energy of another person before, but probably didn't realize it at the time. Have you ever been doing something, when all of a sudden, without looking, you knew someone was behind you? And you turned around and there was someone there. This person was entering your energy field with his (or her) energy field and you felt him before seeing him.

Preparation and Materials

- You will need approximately 30 minutes for the following reflective exercise.
- You will also need your notebook and a pen or pencil.

Activity G

This is an activity to reflect on and write your feelings down in your notebook or journal. Think about a time when you were a child and were scared or hurt and came running to your parents for comfort.

1. Do you remember them embracing you in their loving arms until you felt better? They were showing their love for you by physically holding you. As they wrapped their arms around you, you were also being embraced by their energy bodies.

2. Do you remember feeling the warm healing energy and love their bodies were giving to you?

3. Did you begin to feel much better as a result of this? Were you soon able to go back to what you were doing feeling refreshed and happy?
   Write about how you experienced the energy body.

Activity H

Try these simple exercises to feel your own energy or spiritual body.

1. Begin by rubbing your palms together to warm up your hands. Next, hold both hands, palms facing one another out in front of you, about 6 inches apart. Begin moving your palms slowly in and out decreasing and increasing the space between them. You are building up the energy between your hands.

Can you feel it? Does it feel warm?

2. Now, bring your hands further apart, about 8-10 inches. Begin to bring them slowly back together until you feel a pressure forcing you to expend a little more energy to push them together. They should be no more than 2 inches apart. You are now feeling the etheric level of your aura. Can you feel the buildup of energy between your palms? Can you make an energy ball? What does that feel like?

Activity I

For this activity, make sure your hands are warm, and bring your hands, palms facing each other, a distance of about 7 inches apart. Now point your right index finger at the palm of your left hand. It should be no more than 2 inches away from your palm. Draw some circles on the palm to which your finger is pointing.

Can you feel sensations on that palm? What does it feel like?

Preparation and Materials

- You will need two or more people, a chair and 15-30 minutes, depending on how many people participate in this activity.
- To set up this activity, you will sit in the chair (or on the floor) with your eyes closed and the other person will stand about 8-10 feet behind you.

Activity J

Tell the other person when you are ready and she will approach you very slowly. When you feel the energy field of that person enter your field, raise your hand. Try this several times and then let everyone have a turn sitting in the chair.

What did it feel like when the person entered your field? After several turns, did your perception of the other person's field of energy entering yours happen more quickly?

Objective

- To learn through other people Who You Really Are

Preparation and Materials

This activity will require one or more people, about 30 minutes, and your notebook to record your words or phrases.

Activity K

Ask a few of your trusted and loving friends to help you with this activity. To begin, you will sit or lie down as they surround you in a circle. Close your eyes and listen as each one of your friends takes a turn and uses a word or phrase to describe something about you. Do several rounds of this until you have approximately 20-25 descriptions. Examples: You are a Good Friend, Lovable, Kind, Soaring Spirit, Beacon of Light, Free Spirit, You are Generous

You will also ask one person to record each of the descriptions for you. After doing this activity, reflect on these questions:

Do your friends see something about you that you have never seen? How does that make you feel about yourself? How does that make you feel about them? Do you see God reflecting back to you in each one of your friends?

It will also be fun if everyone gets to have a turn in the center while everyone uses words to describe them.

Chapter 3 Questions

Write the answers to these questions in your notebook. There is no right or wrong answer. These are for your reflection on what you have learned in the chapter.

Are you equal to God? Explain by listing all the ways that you are equal to God.

What was the last thing you remember creating using thought, word or deed?

Can you operate outside of the laws of the universe?

What does it mean to be a "Three Fold Being?"

What can you do to keep your energy or spiritual body functioning properly?

Can you think, speak and act as the God that you are?

Further Study:

Study more about your Energy or Spiritual Body by learning more about how to channel the healing Reiki energy. You may want to read the book *Essential Reiki* by Diane Stein.

According to Dr. Norma Milanovich and Dr. Shirley McCune, in their book, *The Light Shall Set You Free,* there is more to our existence that we cannot see. There are actually nine energy bodies that compose the human energy system, the physical body and eight other electronic fields that circle the human body. These bodies are hidden in the ancient Quabalah or that which is known as the "Tree of Life." I suggest that you study more about this "Tree of Life" (Quabalah) in the many books available.

I also recommend Alex Grey's book *Sacred Mirrors* to view the energy bodies in action.

Questionnaire

Write the answers in your notebook. These questions are to assist you in recognizing your personal growth after reading the chapter.

What have you learned about yourself after doing these activities?

What feelings did you have during the chapter activities?

Did you change in any way after reading Chapter 3 and doing the activities?
If yes, How?

How have you changed the way you relate to others after reading this chapter?

Conversations with God
– *an uncommon dialogue* –

Chapter 4

Summary

Do you wake up in the morning thinking about what kind of "discoveries" you will have that day? Are you "trying to find yourself?" In chapter 4, God tells you life is a creation not a discovery. In fact, you are creating your life every minute of every day. You are a co-creator with God. The $64,000 question is – are you creating it consciously or unconsciously? The key is awareness. If you are moving through life using the tools of creation that God has given you, (thought, word and deed or action) to create your reality, you are making things happen for you and you are in command of your life. However, if you are sleepwalking through your life, life will move you!

You have the power and the ability, using your God given tools, to change anything you want in your world. This begins with deciding very clearly what you want to think, do and have. Next, throw out all negative thoughts you may be thinking and discipline your powerful mind to focus on nothing except what you want to create. Say what you want out loud with the great "I AM" command that calls forth creative power. Know that your "dream" will be delivered by the universe, and always remember to show your gratitude.

"There is no other way the universe knows how to work. There is no other route it knows to take. The universe responds to 'I am' as would a genie in a bottle."

Conversations with God, Book 1, p. 93

"The Self within the heart is like a boundary which divides the world from That. Wherefore he who has crossed that boundary, and has realized the Self, if he is blind, ceases to be blind; if he is wounded, ceases to be wounded; if he is afflicted, ceases to be afflicted."

Chandogya Upanishad
The Lightworker's Way
Dr. Doreen Virtue, p. 79

Chapter 4 Key Points

- Institutions

- Life is a creation, not a discovery

- All attack is a call for help

- Consciously creating your reality

- Self-Empowerment

- Gratitude

New Spirituality Principles

❖ Thought
❖ Word
❖ Deed
❖ The Eighteenth Remembrance (from *Home with God,* the text)
   "Free choice is the act of pure creation, the signature of God, and your gift, your glory, and your power forever and ever."

"You do not live each day to discover what it holds for you, but to create it. You are creating your reality every minute, probably without knowing it."

Neale Donald Walsch
Conversations with God, Book 1, p. 91

Objectives

- To feel and understand how you create the self-empowering Love you have inside of you.

- To recognize the expansion of that Love when you are with others.

Preparation and materials

You will need some time in your sacred space or any other quiet place to think about these questions. Write the answers and any reflections you have about them in your notebook.

Activity L

1. Think about yourself. Can you move past your body, past your personality, past this space and time and feel God in you? Go into your heart, not the muscle of the heart, but the energy of Love, that quiet place of peace and power.

Can you hear the still voice inside of you? When you listen to that voice inside of you, you are free to be Who You Truly Are! Free to be who you desire to be!

Can you remember a time when you listened to that voice against what others were telling you? How did you feel after making your decision? Did you feel self-empowered? What does it feel like? Did you feel liberated?

2. Think about how everyone is a child of God. Do you see God in the person next to you, and the one in front of you and the one behind you? Where ever you are, you are joined in the Love that you are. And when you come together with another, and recognize the God that is in each other, there is an expansion of that Love.

Can you feel your true self expressing itself? Think about the times that you have been with your family, friends, people in your community, etc. Did you feel that expansion of Love? How did it feel? Did it feel like you?

Objectives

- To understand what you can accomplish with the mind and how amazingly powerful it can be by practicing conscious visualization of chosen goals,
- To use and start to practice integration of the three creative aspects of Being: body, mind and spirit.

Preparation and materials

"The Mind is Humanities' Last Explored Frontier." This is a statement from the book, *"The Light Shall Set You Free"* by Dr. Norma Milanovich and Dr. Shirley McCune. Humanity is just beginning to understand much more about the possibilities of the brain and how very powerful the mind can really be. Neale Donald Walsch says that all creation begins with thought and **"God's plan is for you to create anything – everything you want. In such freedom lies the experience of God being God – and this is the experience for which I created You."**

Conversations with God, Book 1, p.61

You will need your notebook and about 30 minutes.

Activity M

Let your imagination soar, throw out all of your previous beliefs about what your mind is capable of, and list in your notebook all of your highest goals for anything that you want to manifest in your life. Do you believe it's possible for you to be a God?

> *"When your thoughts are clear and steadfast, begin to speak them as truths. Say them out loud. Use the great command that calls forth creative power. I am. Make I-am statements to others. "I am" is the strongest creative statement in the universe. Whatever you think, whatever you say, after the words "I am sets into motion those experiences, calls them forth, brings them to you."*
>
> *Neale Donald Walsch*
> *Conversations with God, Book 1, p. 92,93*

Objectives

- To learn how to create your reality by using the tools of creation (thought, word and deed)

- To evolve your absolute faith that the tools of creation are always at play in what will be accomplished in your life

Preparation and Materials

- You will need your notebook.
- Save about 15 minutes a day in your sacred space.

Activity N

1. Choose something you want to bring into your life (manifest), such as in the previous activity, each week for one month. Do you want a new car, a better job or maybe time to go on a vacation? Be sure to specify clearly what your goal will be and when you want this to happen. Write this down in your journal. Be careful in your wording because the universe will send you exactly what you ask for. If you state that you need a new car, you will receive the need for a new car. However, if you say "I am" getting a new car next month, this is the way to make the strongest creative statement to the universe.

2. Then go to your sacred space, do pranic breathing to bring in the white light and state out loud what your goal is. Visualize having what you asked for at least 15 minutes each day. Imagine that you are picking out that car you want and leaving the dealership lot in it. Feel yourself sitting on the new upholstery of the seats. See yourself driving that new car into your garage, as examples. It is necessary to have absolute faith that your wish will be fulfilled.
Do you believe that it will?

3. Most importantly, take time and give thanks in advance in knowing that the universe will send you what you asked for. This is the biggest key in creating your goals: to be grateful before and for the creation.

4. Now what steps are you going to take to make your dream come true? Are you going to go to your boss and ask what you can do to advance yourself in the company so you can make more money? Or perhaps, is it time to look for another job opportunity? As you continue to use your mind to clearly let the universe know exactly what you want and take the steps to make it happen, you will draw your dream to you.

> *"Harnessing your thoughts, exercising control over them, is not as difficult as it might seem. It is all a matter of discipline. It is a question of intent."*
>
> ~ Neale Donald Walsch
> *Conversations with God, Book 1, p. 93*

Objective

- To learn to send and receive messages with your mind.

Preparations and Materials

This will require a partner. One of you will choose to be the Sender and the other will be the Receiver. Each of you will sit in chairs (or on the floor) across from one another facing together.

Activity O

The Sender will think of a color and try to send that color to the Receiver through the power of his mind. For example: if the Sender is thinking of the color yellow, he might visualize in his mind a bunch of yellow bananas or send the letters Y E L L O W to the Receiver. Concentration and connection to the Receiver is very important. You will be amazed at what the mind can do. After trying this a few times, switch Sender and Receiver. You could also create a similar exercise of sending simple things such as symbols or numbers. Relax and have fun with this!

Activity P

After having success with the above exercises, try a more advanced activity. This will also require a partner and is the same as before, with one Sender and one Receiver. This time sit in your chairs, or on the floor, back to back. The Sender will draw a simple picture on a piece of paper that sits in his lap. This should consist of simple shapes, nothing that is very intricate-maybe a boat on a lake surrounded by trees with the sun shining in the background as an example. The Receiver will also have a piece of paper in his lap. As the Sender is drawing the picture, she should concentrate on sending what she is drawing to the Receiver through the power of her mind and emotions. As the Receiver sees, in his mind and feels what is being sent, he will draw that on his piece of paper. After a few minutes, compare drawings. Do they look similar? Try this exercise several times and you will understand the true power of your mind.

Chapter 4 Questions

Write the answer in your notebook. There is no right or wrong answer. This is for your reflection on what you have learned in the chapter.

How do you give gratitude to God? How often do you do it?

Did someone attack you in some way for apparently no reason recently? What do you think that person needs? How did this attack affect you?

What does "standing in your truth" mean to you?

Why doesn't God feed the hungry, heal the sick and create peace on our planet right now?

What is the great command that calls forth creative power?

Further Study:

You can manifest your reality by using the tools of creation to control your environment, including the weather. All you have to do is access your God self and know and believe that you can effect positive change on the weather. You can read more about this by reading the *Weather Healing Book* by Michael H. Jackson.

Questionnaire

 Write the answers in your notebook. There is no right or wrong answer. These questions are to assist you in recognizing your personal growth after reading this chapter.

What have you learned about yourself after doing these activities?

What feelings did you have during the chapter activities?

Did you change in any way after reading Chapter 4 and doing the activities? If yes, How?

How have you changed in the way you relate to others after reading this chapter?

Conversations with God
– an uncommon dialogue –

Chapter 5

Summary

There is only one true path to God and that is through your heart. There are no Ten Commandments. Do these statements sound strange to you? What do they mean? God tells us in chapter five there is no incorrect religion or belief system to find Him, as long as it is based on Love, and says She would never command us to do anything.

"Who would I command? Myself?"
Conversations with God, Book 1, p. 95

This continues the thread woven through the entire book that, we are all one and we are experiencing *for God*. The Word of God, as given to Moses in the Ten Commitments (not Commandments), answers the question that humanity has asked God since the beginning of time, *"How do we find you and get to heaven?"* God tells us that "heaven" or "Enlightenment" is right here on Earth. There is no place we need to go. We are on a journey to nowhere.

"Enlightenment" is understanding there is no where to go, nothing to do, and nobody you have to be except who you are being right now."
Conversations with God, Book 1, p. 98

If we can take the leap of faith and have this KNOWING, the door to experience it, opens for us. In this knowing, should we renounce all Earthly passions? God explains that self-denial is not necessary, and true masters simply set these passions aside, as they would do with anything for which they no longer have any use. We should not judge what we feel passionate about. We can, however, take a look at our passions and see if they serve us based on Who and What We Want to Be. Do not resist them, because God tells us what we resist in our life, persists. Passion is the path to Self-Realization, which turns being into action and provides the fire to fuel the engine of creation. This is the point of all life and this is why we are here on this planet – to create anything we choose in this eternal moment of NOW.

"You are what your deep, driving desire is.
As your desire is, so is your will.
As your will is, so is your deed.
As your deed is, so is your destiny."

Brihadaranyaka Upanishad
IV.4.5
Remembering Your Soul
Purpose, Karen Bishop, p.92

"Experiencing heaven on Earth does not mean that you will never experience problems, difficulties or emotions. God-Realized people look pretty much the same as anyone else, and they tend to all the normal day-to-day stuff that the rest of us do. God Realized individuals can be laborers or world leaders. What has changed for them is their inner selves and their inner awareness and connection to Spirit. Their intention, direction and purpose for life has evolved and changed. They are consciously leading lives in harmony with the higher purpose of Spirit and God. And they are doing this with their everyday lives. Their inner joy, happiness, and experience of love is not dependent on what is happening in their outer lives, because they have a direct link with Spirit, love and the truths of life."

Soul Never Sleeps
Marian Massie, p. 5

Chapter 4 Key Points:

- The path of the heart is the way to God

- There is no such thing as the Ten Commandments

- You are on a journey to nowhere

- What you resist, persists

- Passion is the path to Self-Realization

- Illusions

- The Eternal Moment of Now

New Spirituality Principles

- ❖ No path to God is more direct than any other path.
- ❖ No religion is the "one true religion."
- ❖ No people are "the chosen people," and no prophet is the "greatest prophet."
- ❖ The New Gospel: "We are all one."
- ❖ It is the desire of All That Is to Know Itself in its own Experience. This is the reason for all of Life.
- ❖ Ninth of the Eighteen Remembrances from Home with God: "Free Choice is the act of pure creation, the signature of God, and your gift, your glory, and your power forever."

"Every heart which earnestly asks, Which is the path to God? Is shown. Each is given a heartfelt Truth. Come to Me along the path of your heart, not through a journey of your mind. You will never find Me in your mind."

~ Neale Donald Walsch
Conversations with God, Book 1, p. 94

Objective

- To understand that the way to God and everything else in your world is through your heart (Love) not through your mind.

Preparation and Materials

You will need time in your sacred space
Use your notebook to write your answers in and take some time to contemplate the statement in the objective above.

Activity Q

1. Begin this activity by going to your sacred space and doing your pranic breathing. Bring the white light down into your heart center and think about the love and open heart you have for your husband or wife, your children or an especially good friend.

2. Answer these:
What does that love feel like?
When you feel it does your body feel as light as a feather?
Does this love emanate from that part of you that is God?
Do you feel like smiling from the inside?

3. Now think of a time when your heart was hurting due to a loss of someone close to you, a disappointment or any other similar situation. Do you feel pain in the area of your heart? Does your heart feel closed down? Did your smile disappear?

4. Can you now go back and think of the first part of this activity when you felt that wonderful love? Think about how you felt before. Can you open your heart again and feel that love? How do you feel now? Is this a feeling you would like to sustain for as long as possible? How can you accomplish that?

> *"You shall know that you have taken the path to God, and you shall know that you have found God, for there will be these signs, these indications, these changes in you."*
>
> *Conversations with God, Book 1,* p. 96

Objective

- To find the path Home to God by learning and recognizing the changes in you or signs described in the Ten Commitments given to humanity.

Preparation and Materials

- Go back and review the Ten Commitments on pages 96 and 97, in *Conversations with God, Book 1.*
- Poster board, drawing tools, glue stick, anything you want to use to decorate your Ten Commitments.
- You will need your notebook to write the answers to some questions at the end of the activity.

Activity R

Use your creativity to make a board to display The Ten Commitments. Write or type each of the "complete" commitments and paste them on the poster board. Add your own creative touches and put it in your sacred space.

How are these different from what you originally learned about the Ten Commandments?

Do these make more sense to you?

Do you believe God will punish you if you do not adhere to the Commitments?

Objective

- To identify, focus, and manifest your passions

Preparation and Materials

Poster board, glue stick, scissors, and magazines or other pictures
Notebook for listing your ideas

> *"Passion is the fire that drives us to express who we really are."*
> Neale Donald Walsch
> *Conversations with God, Book 1,* p. 101

Activity S

1. Look through magazines, etc. for pictures of things that you are passionate about. Answer these:

    a) Does one picture, or word or phrase speak to you without knowing why at that moment? Cut out all pictures which represent your passions and glue them to a piece of poster or foam core board. Use your imagination and be creative with this!

    b) Do you want to do some drawing of your passions on the board as well?

    c) What is it that you want the universe to bring to you? Complete your dream board and then ask for your dreams to come true and thank the universe for bringing them to you.

2. Place your dream board where you can see it everyday. Now list ideas of how you can begin to make your dreams come true. Do one thing every day to make your dreams a reality.

Chapter 5 Questions

Write the answers to these questions in your notebook. There is no right or wrong answer. This is for your reflection on what you have learned in the chapter.

Is there something you are resisting in your life? How have you made those things real? How can you remove them?

What does living your life without expectation mean to you?

When you love someone, do you EXPECT to be loved back?

Further Study: To understand more about emotional awareness, read *The Heart of the Soul* by Gary Zukav.

Questionnaire

Write the answers in your notebook. These questions are to assist you in recognizing your personal growth after reading this chapter.

What have you learned about yourself after doing these activities?

What feelings did you have during the chapter activities?

Did you change in any way after reading Chapter 5 and doing the activities?
If yes, How?

How have you changed in the way you relate to others after reading this chapter?

Conversations with God
– an uncommon dialogue –

Chapter 6

Summary

Do you have to suffer through life? God tells the book's author in this chapter that suffering is not necessary and the tools have been given to you to end this pain you put yourself through.

God does not enjoy seeing you suffer, and wants you to know that what occurs in your life merely happens (events are occurrences in time and space which you produce out of choice, and God never interferes with choices). Your reaction to them is what causes the pain.

"I have given you the tools with which to respond and react to events in a way which reduces – in fact, eliminates – pain, but you have not used them."

Conversations with God, Book 1, p. 103

It is important to note that events can be altered or changed if enough people in what is known as the "collective consciousness" have a shift in attitude. Wouldn't that be amazing? The world we live in would be like "Heaven on Earth!"

What are these tools that can stop suffering? Those are the same tools of creation that have been talked about before in previous chapters. Also, In order to avoid suffering and pain, it is necessary to understand that what we focus on is made real. A true Master does not speak about any of his suffering and does not judge self or others. If you are suffering in your life, you are trying to remember the way of God. And, of course, you are God. Therefore, through these painful experiences, you are once again learning Who You Really Are.

He discovers that all pain is unreal.
He no longer can even imagine the state of suffering.

The Light Shall Set You Free
Paramahansa Yogananda
p. 41

Chapter 6 Key Points

- Suffering is not necessary

- Laws of cause and effect

- Collective consciousness

- What you focus on becomes real

- Judgments keep you from joy

- Expectations make you unhappy

- Dis-ease

- There is no right or wrong

New Spirituality Principles

❖ Awareness

❖ The Sixth Remembrance: (from *Home with God*)
"You and God are One. There is no separation between you."

❖ The Eighth Remembrance: (from *Home with God*)
"You cannot change Ultimate Reality, but you can change your experience of it."

> *"You see, suffering has nothing to do with events, but with one's reaction to them.*
> *What's happening is merely what's happening. How you feel about it is another matter."*
>
> Neale Donald Walsch
> *Conversations with God, Book 1,* p. 105

Objectives

- To learn through self reflection that your decision making process that has caused suffering in your life.

- To learn about the Law of Rhythm and how to use the tools from God to alleviate all suffering.

Preparation and Materials

Think about these paragraphs defining the Universal Law of Rhythm.
This information will provide a clear understanding of this inevitable law that governs the physical, mental and emotional planes in our universe. For every high there will be a low in equal measure. By utilizing the tools of creation, you can learn to use the Law of Rhythm to manage the extreme rhythms in your life.
You will need your notebook and something to write with for this activity.

Law of Rhythm

The universe moves in a cyclical fashion, with energy flowing one way and then the other. This movement is defined as the rhythm of the universe, and this rhythm is found in all things. It is called the Law of Rhythm.

The principles underlying this law are defined as the movements of the in-breath and the out-breath of God. Life moves in cycles and is constantly renewing itself, first from the highs and then from the lows, next from within and then from without. These rhythmic motions are what constitute the heartbeat and the pulse of life itself.

The Law of Rhythm basically states that all things move in a cyclical fashion, like the pendulum swinging first to the right and then to the left. The tides flow in and the tides flow out; the sun rises and the sun sets. These rhythms constitute an order of renewal in the universe that can be either disruptive or pleasant, depending upon how one wishes to perceive these rhythms.

Like the physical plane, the mental and spiritual planes also have rhythms. Thus, individuals witness mood shifts and states of mental imbalance. These periods constitute some of the most difficult times that people experience, for the extremes drain individuals of precious energy and serve to lessen the mastery they command over their own mental and emotional bodies.

"For every high, there shall be a low. This is the Law of Rhythm. This is the only law the individual cannot learn to control. The only way in which one can command mastery over it is through mastering one's own emotional and mental states at all times. Doing so allows one to rise above this."

The Light Shall Set You Free, p. 236, 237
Dr. Norma Milanovich
Dr. Shirley McCune

"Everything flows out and in; everything has its tides; all things rise and fall, the measure of the swing to the right, is the measure of the swing to the left; rhythm compensates."

The Kybalion
The Light Shall Set You Free, p. 234
Dr. Norma Milanovich and
Dr. Shirley McCune

Activity T

1. Think about a time in your life when you were "on top of the world!" Answer:

- o Can you remember when you received the highest grade on a test in school?
- o Maybe it was a time when that special someone called you on the phone.
- o Or did your boss pay you a compliment on a job well done?
- o Did you win an athletic competition? Perhaps, it was when your little girl or boy looked up at you with a bright smile on their face and said "I love you!"
- o Whenever it was, do you remember how extremely happy you were? You probably jumped up and down or just felt really excited inside. Think of several times like the examples above when you were so happy and write about these in your notebook.

2. Now think of a time when you were equally unhappy. Answer:
   o Did you ever just have one of those days when nothing seemed to go right and you were so low?
   o Or did you have an argument with someone you love and you became angry and bitter?
   o Did something happen to you that you didn't expect and you ended up in a confused and saddened state? Think about those times and write about them in your notebook.

3. These extremes, in the examples above and the personal experiences you wrote in your notebook, sometimes can be very difficult to go through and can drain your body's energy. How did you feel after the high experience?
How did you feel after the low experience?

When you thoroughly enjoy your life and are filled with excitement, you will also see the extreme low, for as the pendulum swings from the right and back to the left, the opposite event or experience is brought to you. The only way to rise above this law of nature is to consciously control your mental and emotional states. And you can choose not to experience the low.

What you can learn to do is "stay in your center" or "middle of the road" of these mood shifts, never becoming too excited about good things or too unhappy about negative things. This may sound a little strange, especially regarding the happy emotions; however, if you can learn to control the highs, the swing of the pendulum in the opposite direction will not be so extreme.

4. In the next part of this activity, you can now begin to master the highs and lows in your life. The next time you experience a high, enjoy it, but be sure to remember about the "swing of the pendulum." Write about this happy time in your notebook. When a low comes along, write down all the details again in your notebook. Continue to write all highs and lows down in your notebook for a period of three months.

5. After the three months, go back and look at all of your high and low experiences. Reflect back on the highs and lows before you started this activity.
Answer:
   o Do you remember the extremes?
   o Have you learned to "stay in your center?"
   o Have the low times become better?
   o Have you discovered an inner joy that has nothing to do with outside influences?

Activity U

Using your journal, think about and record the decisions you have made in the past that were based on personal beliefs, societal beliefs, and others that have caused you to suffer. Answer:
  o What judgments and expectations regarding self and others caused that suffering for you?
  o Why do you think you suffered?

Activity V

Laughter Exercise - Reduce Stress in Your Life and Help you Stay Centered

The exercise can be done alone or with two or more people. (The more, the merrier, so to speak!) If you are alone, this can be done in your sacred space. However, the exercise can be accomplished almost anywhere you choose.

1) Look at yourself in a mirror or face another person.
2) Inhale deeply through your nose all the way down to your root chakra (bottom of your spine). Then laugh right out loud and continue laughing. If working with another person, the first one who laughs wins! There really is no reason to make this a competition.
3) The first one to laugh will begin to release all the stresses and burdens they have been carrying around. So in a sense, they do win!
4) Laugh by yourself or with another as heartily and as long as you can. You won't know how good it feels until you try it!

Chapter 6 Questions

Write the answer in your notebook. There is no right or wrong answer. This is for your reflection on what you have learned in the chapter.

How can you contribute to a higher vibration of mass consciousness?

According to Gary Zukav in *"The Heart of the Soul,"* p. 269, *"people judge one another because it is easier to believe that someone else is responsible for their circumstances than it is to face the pain of their circumstances."* He continues by saying *"Until you can acknowledge that you possess the same characteristics you judge harshly in others, you will become enraged, disappointed, angry, and contemptuous when you see them in others."*

Do you judge yourself?

Do you judge other people?

Have you been judged by someone for something they did not like about you? How did that make you feel?

How can you find joy in your life?

For Further Study:

Study more about the Law of Rhythm and the other Universal Laws that God has given you in *The Light Shall Set You Free*, by Dr. Norma Milanovich.and Dr. Shirley McCune

Questionnaire

Write the answers in your notebook. These questions are to assist you in recognizing your personal growth after reading this chapter.

What have you learned about yourself after doing these activities?

What feelings did you have during the chapter activities?

Did you change in any way after reading Chapter 6 and doing the activities? If yes, How?

How have you changed in the way you relate to others after reading this chapter?

Conversations with God
– an uncommon dialogue –

Chapter 7

Summary

Are you in the spiritual game? God tells Neale Donald Walsch that being in the "spiritual game" means dedicating your whole mind, your whole body and your whole soul to the process of creating Self in the image of God. This conscious creation is a day to day, hour by hour, moment by moment act of supreme consciousness. And the key to success of this process is not being attached to the results. That's a pretty tall order!

 However, if you are "in the game," and in your God space, you will find peace of mind and release from the struggle of life. Then the creative ideas will flow and this is what life is all about. God wants exactly what you want, and this comes to us through cause and effect. If you desire, as the author did in the book, to do more than survive on a day to day basis, begin NOW to open your heart to listen, really listen to what God is trying to tell you. He is speaking to you.

You are responsible for only you and no other human soul, and if there are those who are dependent on you, it is your responsibility to make them independent as soon as possible. God explains that

"You are no blessing to them so long as they need you to survive, but bless them truly only in the moment they realize you are unnecessary."
Conversations with God, Book 1, p.114

Therefore, God's greatest moment is the moment you, who are His/Her children, realize that you need no God. Are you in the spiritual game?

"When you follow Me, the struggle disappears. Live in your God space and the events become blessings, one and all."

Conversations with God, Book 1, p. 115

"Every Cause has its Effect;
every Effect has its Cause;
everything happens according to Law;
Chance is a name for a Law not recognized;
There are many planes of causation,
but nothing escapes The Law."

The Kybalion
p. 38

Chapter 7 Key Points

- The "Spiritual Game"

- Self-Realization

- God's payoff

- You need no God

- Conscious co-creation

- Law of Cause and Effect

New Spirituality Principles

- ❖ Tomorrow's God is needless.

- ❖ Tomorrow's God will be unconditionally loving, nonjudgmental, non-condemning, and non-punishing

> *"This is a day-to-day, hour to hour, moment – to-moment act of supreme consciousness. It is a choosing and a re-choosing every instant. It is ongoing creation. Conscious creation. Creation with a purpose. It is using the tools of creation we have discussed, and using them with awareness and sublime intention."*
>
> Neale Donald Walsch
> *Conversations with God, Book 1,* p.113

Objective

- To determine whether you are living day to day in your God space and using the tools God has given you for conscious creation. This is called being in the "Spiritual Game."

Preparation and Materials

Review Chapter 7 in the book and think about what being in the "Spiritual Game" means to you.

Activity W

1. Make columns in your notebook or use this table:

Ways I Am In the Spiritual Game	Ways I Am Not in the Spiritual Game	"Ways I Will Change"

If you are consciously in the Spiritual Game, your God space, you will know what is important to you and set goals to achieve those things you want. What are some of your goals? What steps are you taking to achieve them?

However, if you live your life only responding to the events going on around you and never think about what it is that you really want, you are not in the spiritual game. Do some of your decisions reflect this? If so, you have become a victim of the results of the Universal Law of Cause and Effect.

This law states that nothing happens by chance outside the Universal Laws. Have you heard people say, nothing happens by accident? They were correct! Every thought we have, every action that we take, has its direct and indirect impact on the events which are part of the chain of cause and effect. You have free will to act with right action or wrong action in your behavior towards yourself and others. Choosing right action, such as forgiveness and unconditional love, will move you up the ladder towards God, and wrong action, such as holding on to old grievances, will move you away from being like God. Which result do you want to achieve?

2. Under the captions in the chart above or in your notebook, list all the ways that you believe you are taking part in the spiritual game and then, in the other column, list all the ways you are not consciously in the game. Then in the third column, under the Ways I Will Change, list all the changes you can make to get back in the game. Then release all those things that no longer serve you, using intention or through the ceremony in Chapter 2.

Do you feel more tuned in to the Spiritual Game Now? Are you letting God flow through you?

> *"Let your love propel your beloveds into the world – and into the full experience of who they are. In this will you have truly loved."*
> Neale Donald Walsch
> *Conversations with God, Book 1, p. 115*

Objective

- To assist you in preparing your loved ones for their independence from you

Preparation and Materials

You will need about 30 minutes and your notebook to record the answers to the questions.

Activity X

Assisting children to assume their independence from parents

1. Reread Chapter 7 in the book and pay particular attention to pages 114-115. The author is told by God "Your job is to render them independent; to teach them as quickly and completely as possible how to get along with out you."

2. Now think about those who are dependent on you for their survival.

Dependent Activities	Ways to Become Independent

3. Make a list of how they are dependent on you.

4. Answer:

- o How can you help each one of these people on the road to becoming independent from you?
- o Do you think this is a good idea?
- o Now, devise a long term plan on how to bless them with their independence.

Chapter 7 Questions

Write the answer in your notebook. There is no right or wrong answer. This is for your reflection on what you have learned from the chapter.

According to the book, "God's greatest moment is the moment when you realize you need no God." p.114 Do you need God?

What is the object of your life?

How did your parents render you independent from them?

When did you feel you could survive without their help?

Do you ever feel separated from God?

Do you feel you need to be saved? If yes, from what?

Do you feel guilty for wanting to change something that is not working in your life?

Further Study:

Read more about the Laws of Cause and Effect in *The Kybalion.*

Questionnaire

Write the answers in your notebook. These questions are to assist you in recognizing your personal growth after reading the chapter.

What have you learned about yourself after doing these activities?

What feelings did you have during the chapter activities?

Did you change in any way after reading Chapter 7 and doing the activities?
If yes, How?

How have you changed in the way you relate to others after reading this chapter?

Conversations with God
– an uncommon dialogue –

Chapter 8

Summary

What is another way to learn Who You Really Are? The answer is through all your relationships with people, places and events. God tells the reader in this chapter that most romantic relationships are entered into for the wrong reason and that is why they are doomed to fail. You believe by loving another you are lovable. However, the first step to loving another, is in loving yourself. The purpose of the sacred sacrament of marriage is not for another to complete you, but to have another with whom you might share in YOUR COMPLETENESS.

"The purpose of a relationship is to decide what part of yourself you'd like to see "show up," not what part of another you can capture and hold."
Conversations with God, Book 1, p.122

The great paradox is: You have no need for a particular other in order for you to experience fully Who You Are, and without another you are nothing.

And let the Light into our hearts and minds,
the whole world becomes alive.

The world is a lovely garden,
full of dreams, life, and beauty.
It is a special place shared by many kingdoms,
And the one place where all can connect
And grow together."

The Light Shall Set You Free
Dr. Norma Milanovich
Dr. Shirley McCune, p. 365

Chapter 8 Key Points

- Bless all your relationships

- Relationships help you know Who You Really Are

- The most loving person is the person who is self-centered

- If you cannot love yourself, you cannot love another

- The purpose of life is for the soul to evolve

- The Highest Good for you becomes the Highest Good for another

- You have no obligations in all of life

- Opportunity is the cornerstone of religion, the basis of all spirituality

- You are a messenger

New Spirituality Principles

❖ Every human being is as special as every other human being who has ever lived, lives now, or ever will live.

❖ You are all messengers, every one of you is carrying a message to life about life every day, every hour every moment.

❖ Awareness

❖ Responsibility

❖ Honesty

❖ Gratitude

> *"The soul has come to the body, and the body to life, for the purpose of evolution. You are evolving, you are becoming. And you are using your relationship with everything to decide what you are becoming."*
> Neale Donald Walsch
> *Conversations with God, Book 1,* p. 126

Objective

▪ To see how everyone and everything in this world is a unique expression and messenger of God.

Preparation and Materials

Read the next activity completely before you begin this activity since you will need to visualize most of it while you are in a meditative state. You can also record this meditation and listen to it.

After the visualization meditation, write the answers to the questions in your notebook.

Activity Y
Note: You may wish to record this mediation and play it back to allow yourself the full affect...

1. Go to your sacred space or any other place where you can be alone and bring yourself into a meditative state through your pranic breathing process. Now visualize yourself watching a beautiful snowfall as all the flakes blow here and there as they travel through the air and fall to the ground.

Answer:
- o Do you see the ones that are a little bigger than the others? That one was a different shape.
- o Did you see it? There are some smaller ones!
- o Did you see them? Now there are some of sleet and snow mixed together. Each one is unique. However, they are all beautiful snowflakes! Now see them all take their individual place in the white blanket that covers the Earth.
- o Do you see how this pristine white blanket makes outside look so bright?

2. Now, still in your meditative state, visualize yourself standing on the side of a street watching people going by in a fun parade. Oh! Look, there is a beauty queen sitting on a float! Isn't she beautiful! Did you see the very tall man with the little dog? There is a big man with his cheeks all puffed out playing a tuba in the band marching down the street. Look at the colorful costumes the ladies from Mexico are wearing. There is a little person dressed up like a baby carrying a large baby bottle. Visualize yourself waving and applauding to the different people (you can visualize anything you want in the parade) as the parade ends and goes down the street. They were all so unique and beautiful!

3. Take a few minutes to come out of your meditation and back to an alert state. Now think about the snowflakes you saw in your meditation. Do you remember how different each one looked as it drifted to the ground? They were all unique! Yet they were all beautiful snowflakes! Now think about all the different people you saw performing in the parade. They were quite unique, weren't they? Yet, they were all beautiful people!

Just like you, each one of the people you saw in the parade has a spark of God's Light inside of them. And everyone on this planet has that God Light too! Some have very bright sparks and others have dim sparks that you can barely see. As each individual opens their heart to receive more and more of this God Light, just like the snowfall that makes everything so bright, the God sparks in people will blanket the Earth with Light!

4. Self-Reflection Do you see everyone on the planet, no matter what they look like on the outside, as beautiful God sparks? Visualize looking down from an airplane at night and seeing all sparks of God in the people on the planet. Do you consider these people to be part of your Earth family?

> *"It is only through your relationships with other people, places and events that you can even exist (as a knowable quantity, as an identifiable something) in the universe."*
>
> Neale Donald Walsh
> *Conversations with God, Book 1,* p. 121

> "The rounded world is fair to see,
> Nine times folded in mystery:
> Through baffled seers cannot impart
> The secret of its laboring heart,
> Throb thine with Nature's throbbing breast,
> And all is clear from east to west.
> Spirit that lurks each form within
> Beckons the spirit of its kin;
> Self-kindled every atom glows
> And hints the future which it owes."
>
> Ralph Waldo Emerson
> Nature
> Nature Speak, Ted Andrews
> p. 13

Objectives

- To connect with the Nature Kingdom and realize, through observation and experiential exercises, how wonderful and refreshing it is to receive the many spiritual blessings it has to offer.

- You will understand that everything in God's Kingdom is a part of God.

Activity Z
Overview

One of these relationships that many people have long forgotten and taken for granted is humanity's relationship with Mother Nature. Her sacred kingdom has a consciousness, a heartbeat, a purpose, just as we do. In fact, without this vital symbiotic relationship humanity would cease to survive. Everything our bodies need comes from the gifts from God through the Nature Kingdom. The foods we eat, medicines we take when we are ill, and our precious oxygen are just a few things that are provided for us. As we exhale and give off harmful carbon dioxide, the plant kingdom takes that into its system and thrives on it. Plants in turn, through the process of photosynthesis, produce the oxygen we breathe. This kingdom provides our prana, chi, our elixir of life. Without this sacred kingdom, humanity would not survive.

Preparation and Materials

You will need a journal or notebook and something to write with. It is not necessary, but you may want to carry a book that can identify species of plants, trees, shrubs and flowers.

Activity AA

1. Plan to go to a place where you can spend as much time as possible in nature. Perhaps there is a walking trail in a forest nearby, or maybe there is a park you can visit. Just as in your sacred place, being in nature will shift your focus from the physical world to the magic and wonder of the Divine in you. As you step, let your feet ground and connect you to the Earth.

2. Plan to do some deep breathing to energize your body and bring it to a more alert state. If it's warm enough, take your shoes and socks off and let your feet feel the coolness of the grass, the soft bed of pine needles that cover the floor of the forest, or the hardness of the terrain. Really begin to connect with your Beautiful Mother.

3. Answer deeply: What is calling out for you to notice? Record everything in your notebook.

4. Now as you walk, use all six of your senses – sight, hearing, taste, touch, smell and your intuition. See the many colors of green in the landscape. Green is the color of abundance, renewal and healing. Take all of this in through your senses. How do you feel in this environment?

5. Listen to the many natural sounds you hear. Answer:
    o Are there birds singing, bees buzzing or squirrels cracking nuts open in the trees?
    o Do you hear the sound of your footsteps as you move through the floor of the forest?
    o Are you hearing things you missed before?
    o Do you feel as though you are in another sacred space?
    o Is there a clean natural brook or stream nearby? Taste the cool, clear, life-giving water. Perhaps you see honey suckle growing close by.
    o Why not taste the golden drops as you did when you played outside as a child? Let your inner child come out to play!

6. Now touch and see how many different textures you can feel and record this in your journal. Let your fingers trace the veins in the leaves and feel the roughness of the tree bark. How does it feel to touch this wonderful weave of nature?

7. What do you smell? Maybe it's the soil of the Earth, the scent of flowering jasmine in the air, or the spruce trees growing just up ahead. Feel your sense of wonder and awe of this magical place come to the surface. Let your intuition guide you into the other

realms where you are aware of the nature spirits. Honor this sacred kingdom and take time to sit and meditate while you are here. Feel yourself as ONE with nature and ask this kingdom to communicate with you.

8. Summary Reflection: Record everything in your journal. Do you feel your relationship with Mother Nature has been renewed?

Objective

- To connect with the animal kingdom and understand, through observation and experiential activities, the joy and spiritual blessings a relationship such as this can provide.

Preparation and Materials

You will need your notebook for reflection and to answer the questions.
You will need your favorite pet, or a friend's pet and about 30 minutes.
If you have a camera, ask a friend to take a picture of you and your pet to remember this special time.

Activity BB

Exploring your relationship with the animal kingdom

1. Sit beside your pet in a comfortable place where there are no distractions for either of you. This is a time to really tune in and connect with your sweet dog, cat, bunny, horse, ferret, etc.

2. Stroke your pet and feel the texture. Is it soft like silk? Maybe it's a little rough. Now stroke your pet again. How does he respond to your affection? Does she like it? Did your pet give you a little kiss? How did its tongue feel? Was it wet, soft, smooth, or rough? Gently touch your pet's nose.
What did that feel like? Was it hot, cold, and a little slimy? How did your pet react when you touched its nose?

Just like humans, pets have energy or spiritual bodies too. When you touch your pet with your hand, he feels your energy as well. This will be very comforting to your animal. Stroke your pet in different areas of his body. How does he respond to that? Remember from previous activities that you have healing energy radiating from your hands.

3. Now look at your pet's eyes. Aren't they beautiful? Do they look back at you? Ask to connect with your pet's soul. Animals have souls too. What does it say to you? Spend time sending love to your pet. Treasure this special time with your pet and thank your pet for all the joy he has added to your life.

Objective

- To look at the relationship you are having with yourself and take the time to "tune in" and do something nice for just you.

Preparation and Materials

You will need your notebook, something to write with and some time you can set aside for yourself at least once a week, or more if possible.

Activity CC

Taking care of self !

1. When was the last time you did something nice for yourself?

2. Take the time several times a week to do something nice, a little favor for you. Do this for one month and record what you did each time for yourself in your notebook.

3. How do you feel about doing something just for you?

4. Do you feel worthy? Articulate further to yourself and make your feelings clearer in words; scribe those feelings.

Chapter 8 Questions

Write the answers in your notebook. There is no right or wrong answer. This is for your reflection on what you have learned in the chapter.

Bless all relationships! Do you now feel more tuned in to your relationship with all God's Kingdoms? (The Animal Kingdom, the Nature Kingdom, and the Kingdom of Humanity) How are all of these Kingdoms related to one another?

Do you understand how every person on the planet carries their own Light?
How can you make your Light brighter? How can you help others to brighten their Light?

What relationships have you had or are currently having that contributed to you knowing Who You Really Are?
Make a List.

What did you learn about yourself from them?

How did these relationships help you heal a part of your soul?

Did they teach you fear or love?

What opportunities did they provide?

You are a messenger. What message are you sending to the universe?

Further Study:

Another kingdom that Humanity has a relationship with that you might want to study, is the Mineral Kingdom. Crystals come from the Mineral Kingdom. These crystals are built from one of seven possible geometric forms and each has their own esoteric properties.

Questionnaire

Write the answers in your notebook. These questions are to assist you in recognizing your personal growth after reading this chapter.

What have you learned about yourself after doing these activities?

What feelings did you have during the chapter activities?

Did you change in any way after reading Chapter 8 and doing the activities? If yes, How?

How have you changed in the way you relate to others after reading this chapter?

Conversations with God
– an uncommon dialogue –

Chapter 9

Summary

How have you created yourself? Are you SELF created or have you let others decide Who You Are? These questions are explored in this chapter. The author tells you that God has given you this delicious life to experience anything you want as many times as you want, and there are absolutely no "right" or "wrong" decisions. You will never be punished by God for anything, absolutely anything you do.

This sounds like the perfect set up, so why are you giving your power away to others? When others tell you how you should feel about something and that doesn't resonate with you, something deep inside tells you what others have told you is not Who You Are. Have you ever done something and felt bad about it afterwards? You will find that uncomfortable feeling is telling you that you are blocking your true God – Self.

In order for your soul to evolve, (and that is exactly what it wants to do) thinking is absolutely necessary. Thinking and making decisions for YOURSELF is not easy and you may find yourself alone on this path without approval from others. Why, indeed, should you take this harder path? Because this is the only game in town God tells the book's author. If you play "the game" of life CONSCIOUSLY and with AWARENESS, everything gets better and soon you will be living a life full of JOY.

"Yet, what is 'right'? Can you be truly objective in these matters? Or are 'right' and 'wrong' simply descriptions overlaid on events and circumstances by you, out of your decision about them?"

Conversations with God, Book 1, p. 152

"On this planet, you react and live from what you believe. You cannot get away from your beliefs. Every thought is a belief; if you have a mind, you will have beliefs! This is how everyone functions in this dimension. The key to your growth and happiness is what you choose to believe. You have control over your thoughts, and so you have control over your beliefs – thus your realities. No one pours thoughts into your head or tells you to think this or that. You are in total control of your life, but most of us choose not to exercise this control, or we are unaware we have this control."

Soul Never Sleeps
Marian Massie, p. 38

"Good thought will produce good actions and bad thoughts will produce bad actions. Hatred does not cease by hatred at any time; hatred ceases by love."

Buddha
The Light Shall Set You Free
Dr. Norma Milanovich
Dr. Shirley McCune, p. 213

Chapter 9 Key Points

- You cannot fail

- Re-incarnation

- There is no absolute right or wrong

- Thinking for yourself

- Your next highest vision for self

- There is nothing else to do

- Your truth is the only one that matters

New Spirituality Principles

- ❖ There is no such thing as Right and Wrong. There is only What Works and What Does Not Work, depending upon what it is that you seek to be, do, or have.

❖ The Triad Process
1. Nothing in my world is real.
2. The meaning of everything is the meaning I give it.
3. I am who I say I am, and my experience is what I say it is.

❖ Holistic Living Principles
o Awareness
o Honesty
o Responsibility

> *"Such a choice – a decision coming from no previous personal knowledge – is called pure creation. And the individual is aware, deeply aware, that in the making of such decisions is the Self created."*
> Neale Donald Walsch
> p. 154

Objectives

- To learn about the Law of Vibration.

- To become aware and learn to access how you feel.

- To choose behaviors that will help you evolve.

Preparation and Materials

You will need your journal; review the following information:

You know how important it is to take care of your body by eating the most nutritious foods, exercising regularly and other good decisions to keep you in optimum health.

Did you know it is important to also take care of your mind?

How do you do that?

You accomplish this by making a choice to think good thoughts. These thoughts and emotions that we think and feel each have a vibration, such as one that is made when you hit a key on a piano. In fact, everything in this universe has a vibration. This means that all things are moving or oscillating at a certain frequency. Positive thoughts and emotions like love, happiness, gratitude and joy have high vibration. Negative thoughts such as anger, envy, fear, or hate have a low vibration.

Having positive, high vibratory thoughts helps you keep balance in your body and assists your soul in evolving to a higher consciousness, while the negative ones do not help your soul move forward and can actually be harmful to your body.

Through the Universal Law of Vibration you draw that which resides in that frequency. In other words, you draw to you the same vibration that you send out. Like attracts like. You are sending out your vibrations to others. Your thoughts do affect the people around you.

Activity DD

Think about each of the following and write, sketch or even draw or paint your feelings about:

1. Think about the last time you had a happy thought. How did you feel after you had that thought?

2. What did you do after that thought?

3. Now think about the last time you had a negative thought. How did you feel then?

4. What did you do after thinking that thought?

5. Can you feel the difference in the vibration of each thought?

6. Which did you like better?

7. Can you think of a time when people you know were affected by your thoughts and emotions?

8. Was this thought of a high vibration or low vibration?

9. How did they react to you?

10. Can you think of a time when you were affected by what someone was sending out to you?

11. How did you feel?

12. Would you rather be around a person who is optimistic or pessimistic about life?

13. How can you keep your vibrations as high as possible?

14. If more people were optimistic, do you think that would raise the vibration of our planet?

> *"There is no 'right' or 'wrong' in these matters. But by your decisions you paint a portrait of Who You Are."*
>
> Neale Donald Walsch

Preparation and Materials

- Review pages 154 and 155 in the book and think about Who You Were before you read this book.
- Artist paper or canvas (any size you choose)
- Pens or markers, paint brushes, any color of acrylic paints

Activity EE

Painting a "Portrait of Who You Are"

Begin to "Paint your Portrait" by using all the words you can think of to describe "Who You Were" before you read this book. Write all these descriptions of "You" with the pen or marker on the piece of artist paper or canvas. Let the writing dry a bit. Bless all the experiences that brought you to now and that gave you these descriptions of "You" and release them if they no longer serve you. Then paint over these old descriptions of "You" with a paint of any color you choose. Then let this dry completely. When it is dry, write on your canvas words to describe you now. Decorate this "New Portrait of You" any way you want. Be creative and have fun with this activity! Place this "work of art" in your sacred space.

Chapter 9 Questions

Write the answers in your notebook. There are no right or wrong answers. This is for your reflection on what you have learned in the chapter.

Do you try to please others in deference to self?

How have you given your power away to others?

Do you believe in re-incarnation? If yes, what is its purpose?

Do you think you can fail in life?

Think about Who You Are in relation to this statement: "Killing is justified if someone has taken the life of another." What is your opinion?

Further Study:

Learn more about how to take responsibility for the choices you make, and gain control over your life, by reading *The Mind of the Soul* by Gary Zukav.

Questionnaire

Write the answers in your notebook. These questions are to assist you in recognizing your personal growth after reading this chapter.

What have you leaned about your self after doing these activities?

What feelings did you have during the chapter activities?

Did you change in any way after reading Chapter 9 and doing the activities? If yes, How?

How have you changed in the way you relate to others after reading this chapter?

Conversations with God
– an uncommon dialogue –

Chapter 10

Summary

God's Love is UNCONDITIONAL. No matter what you do, God always Loves You. God does not have any conditions or expectations attached to His Love. After eons of conditioning to the contrary, is this hard for you to believe?

You are made of that Divine Light of God. That is your true nature. You are Love and nothing else. That unbounded field of Intelligence, Light and Energy is not outside of you somewhere. It is within you.

This is what Self-Realization is all about. The journey to SELF is not about your individual personality. It is about the completion of your journey back to your God-self, and the awakening realization that you are a part of God.

Do not look outside of yourself for God. Now is the time to wake up and re-member God and feel that which you are! You will know you are love and nothing else. If you let yourself feel that love, you will know it's always been there waiting for you. You will know that you and God are ONE.

"The highest feeling is the experience of unity with All That Is. This is the great return to Truth for which the soul yearns. This is the feeling of perfect love."

Conversations with God, Book 1, p. 83

"What the soul is after is – the highest feeling of love you can imagine. This is the soul's desire. This is its purpose. The soul is after the feeling. Not the knowledge, but the feeling. It already has the knowledge, but knowledge is conceptual. Feeling is experiential. The soul wants to feel itself, and thus to know itself in its own experience."

Conversations with God, Book 1, p. 83

"The only meaning of life is to find the all-loving God, who has kept us apart from Himself by shyly hiding from us.

Paramahansa Yogananda

"Spirit is the essence of consciousness, the energy of the universe that creates all things. Each one of us is a part of that Spirit – a Divine entity. So the Spirit is the Higher Self, the eternal being that lives within us."

Shakti Gawain
The Light Shall Set You Free
Dr. Norma Milanovich
Dr. Shirley McCune, p. 155

Chapter 10 Key Points

- God's Love for You is Unconditional

- God has no expectations for you

- God is not outside of you

- You have God's Divine Light inside of You

- The Soul's Desire is to feel that Perfect Love

- Love is the HIGHEST Answer

New Spirituality Principles

❖ Tomorrow's God is separate from nothing, but is Everywhere Present, the All in All, the Alpha and the Omega, the Beginning and the End, the sum total of Everything that ever was, is now, and ever shall be.

❖ Tomorrow's God will be unconditionally loving, nonjudgmental, non-condemning, and non-punishing.

❖ God needs nothing. God requires nothing in order to be happy. God is happiness itself. Therefore, God requires nothing from anyone or anything in the universe.

"You do not remember the experience of the love of God. And so you try to imagine what God's love must be like, based on what you see of love in the world."

Neale Donald Walsch
p. 17

Objective

▪ To learn how to discern whether love is given by you and others "conditionally" or "unconditionally."

▪ To learn how to discern whether love is received by you and others "conditionally" or "unconditionally."

Preparation and Materials

Think about all the ways you see "Love in Action" in the world around you. You will need your notebook and about one hour per day for about eight days.

Activity FF

1. Make a list in your notebook of all the ways you observe love being expressed for three days.

Date	Love In Action 'Event'	Time of Day

2. After the third day, look at each entry of "love in action" and decide whether this love was expressed unconditionally or conditionally. Answer:

    a) Did someone say or do something out of love only? Or did this person expect something in return for their love?

    b) Did they say "I love you" to someone and expect to hear the same in return?

    c) If they did not get what they wanted, did this person become hurt?

3. The next part of this activity is for you to observe how you "love. Every time you express love during the next three days, write down the situation in your notebook.

Date	How I Have Loved	Time of Day

4. Then after the third day, referring to your entries of how you expressed love, think about whether your love was given freely and in an unconditional way or extended with conditions and expectations. Answer:

    a) If your love was sometimes given with expectations, how did you feel when you did not receive what you wanted in return?

    b) What do you need to do to give love unconditionally more often?

    c) Now, how do you "love" yourself? Is it with conditions and expectations?

    d) Reflect on this and write your feelings in your notebook.

Chapter 10 Questions

Write the answers in your notebook. There is no right or wrong answer. This is for your reflection on what you have learned in the chapter.

Do you feel God's unconditional Love for you? Where do you feel it?

How can you allow more of God's Love and Light into your body?

How do you give unconditional Love?

Is there anyone from whom you have been withholding this unconditional love?

What does "Love is the only answer" mean to you?

Further Study:

The following was quoted by His Holiness the Dalai Lama,

"Pay attention not only to the cultivation of knowledge but to the cultivation of qualities of the heart, so that at the end of education, not only will you be knowledgeable, but also you will be a warm-hearted and compassionate person."

Study more about the Dalai Lama's philosophy regarding compassion of the heart in the book, *Live Life a Better Way*, a collection of his public lectures given in India to audiences from all walks of life.

Questionnaire

Write the answers in your notebook. These questions are to assist you in recognizing your personal growth after reading the chapter.

What have you learned about yourself after doing these activities?

What feelings did you have during the chapter activities?

Did you change in any way after reading Chapter 10 and doing the activities? If yes, How?

How have you changed in the way you relate to others after reading this chapter?

Conversations with God
– an uncommon dialogue –

Chapter 11

Summary

It's time to change your mind about some things! Is your mind filled with your own thoughts about things such as money, time or love, to name just a few, or are they someone else's thoughts? God tells the author that most of your thoughts are based on the experience of others. These root thoughts are not your "true thoughts." They do not serve you and cause confusion in what you want the universe to send to you.

"The wrong thought is your idea about money. You love it, and yet you say it is the root of all evil."

Conversations with God, Book 1, p. 162

The universe receives two thoughts about money and it doesn't know what to do. Also, much of today's society believes that there is never enough of anything that is good. In order to change your life and these "root thoughts," it is necessary to train your mind to think a "New Way." You can change the sponsoring thought and reverse the thought, word, action process. The key is to do the deed (action) you want to have the new thought about and then say the words about your new thought. For example, the "new thought" would be "there is enough of everything." If you act in accordance with this "new thought" and do this before your mind has a chance to think about it, you can teach your mind to think a "New Way."

"New thought is your only chance. It's your only real opportunity to evolve, to grow, to truly become Who You Really Are!"

Conversations with God, Book 1, p. 16

"We do not CHOOSE how we will feel. Instead, thought-forms and attitudes of others permeate our consciousness and we turn our lives over to them by buying into their beliefs, attitudes, emotions, and actions instead of creating our own."

The Light Shall Set You Free
Dr. Norma Milanovich
Dr. Shirley McCune, p. 302

"Einstein understood the concepts that are being discussed here and tried to tell us in a different way. Once a reporter asked him "What is the most important question in the world?" He replied, "The most important question in the world is, do you want a peaceful, happy, abundant world in which to live, or do you want a foreboding, fearful, and scarce world?"

The reporter, slightly puzzled asked, "Why is this the most important question in the world?" Einstein replied, "Because whatever you choose, you will create."

The Light Shall Set You Free
Dr. Albert Einstein, p. 302

"No limits are set for the ascent of man, and to each and everyone the Highest stands open. Here it is only your personal choice that decides."

Hasidic saying
The Light Shall Set You Free
p. 299

Chapter 11 Key Points

- Root Thoughts, Sponsoring Beliefs

- "New Thinking"

- There's Enough

New Spirituality Principles

- ❖ THERE IS ENOUGH

- ❖ The Illusion of Insufficiency (The Ten Illusions in the book: *Home with God*)

- ❖ Tools of Creation:
  Thought   Word   Deed

> *"Do the deed you want to have the new thought about. Then say the words that you want to have your new thought about. Do this often enough and you'll train the mind to think a new way."*
>
> Neale Donald Walch
> p. 164

Objectives

- To learn how to bring more abundance into your life by releasing old mental tapes and "Thinking a New Way."

- To experience this "New Thinking" as bringing more joy into your life.

- You will understand that you can use the tools of creation to create your own reality.

Preparation and Materials

- You will need your notebook.

- Think about how the media floods you with pictures and reports of people in poverty all the time. You can turn on CNN or one of the "all news all the time" channels and see this twenty-four seven if you wish. But why would you want to?

- When you see these images on television or other types of media, they become real in your mind. This brings to you such things as fear and worry about the possibility of your being in poverty too. And this belief that "there isn't enough for everybody" will put you in a state of "poverty consciousness." And your fear and belief in this will keep you from attracting abundance to you. Do you have a sponsoring belief or a "root thought" that people living in poverty will be rewarded in some way by God? It is time to "Think a New Way!" Try the following exercise.

Activity FF

1. For a period of about a week do not watch:
   o T.V. news
   o Listen to the news in any way.

2. Also, it is essential that you not:
   o Read or see the images in newspapers or magazines either.
   o Avoid all these "half full" images and visuals to interfere with your "New Thinking." Please understand that those people you see suffering in poverty have made the choices to experience this. They are all trying to learn Who They Really Are.

3. It is necessary to stop all those "old programs" that keep popping up in your mind that support those root thoughts that God rewards us for being in poverty, as well as other old thoughts you may have.

4. Now visualize and feel that "there is enough" of everything for you and everyone else in the world. Remember, it is a matter of choice and that everything in the physical world is an illusion or what you think it is. Know you are worthy of all abundance.

5. Next, write down your "affirmation" that "There Is Enough of Everything for Everyone." and speak it out loud several times a day. Think only loving positive thoughts.

6. Keep any negative thoughts from lingering in your consciousness. If one comes in, gently thank it for giving you the choice not to dwell on it and let it go!

7. After doing this for a week, go back to paying attention to the media. Compare, by answering the following questions or charting your feelings:

Media Coverage	My Immediate Thoughts	My Feelings

a) How does this make you feel?

b) Do these images and words bring you back to a place of worry and fear about not having enough?

c) Might you consider limiting your exposure to the media?

d) In your understanding that there is "Enough of Everything for Everyone," can you become detached from what you see happening around you?

e) Do you see the "illusion" in your old way of thinking?

Try this "New Thinking" for other things in your world!

Objective

- To find more joy in your life through "New Thinking."

Preparation and Materials

You will need:
- your notebook
- something to write with
- an hour to complete this activity

Activity GG

1. Think about and document:

   a) Do you have root thoughts regarding such things as:

	My Root Thought/Belief	My New Thinking
God		
money		
religion		
love		
sex		
war		

   b) Complete and add to the chart list some "New Thinking" for each topic.

2. Over the next week, add to the above list of your root thoughts or sponsoring beliefs.

3. Consider deeply, do you want to develop "New Thinking" regarding these? Journal for a good long while to bring up any deep seated beliefs you may wish to address and choose to keep or let go.

Chapter 11 Questions

Write the answers in your notebook. There is no right or wrong answer. This is for your reflection on what you have learned from the chapter.

Do you believe that you have to do something to get something in return?

Is there any connection between money inflow and work outflow?

Is there enough abundance for every single person on the planet!

Further Study:

Read Eckhart Tolle's book, *A New Earth*, in which he explains *"Who you think you are is also intimately connected with how you see yourself treated by others."* He is talking about abundance and how you manifest that in your life, and continues by saying, **"***If the thought of lack – whether it be money, recognition, or love – has become part of who you think you are, you will always experience lack.***"** *Read more about this in his book.*

Questionnaire

Write the answers in your notebook. These questions are to assist you in recognizing your personal growth after reading the chapter.

What have you learned about yourself after doing these activities?

What feelings did you have during the chapter activities?

Did you change in any way after reading Chapter 11 and doing the activities? If yes, How?

How have you changed in the way you relate to others after reading this chapter?

Conversations with God
– an uncommon dialogue –

Chapter 12

Summary

Are you living your life in the Being State or the Doing State? Doing happens as a result of producing something with your body. Being is the state that comes about when you listen to your soul. Your soul does not care about what you are doing with your body. The body is an instrument your soul uses to bring forth its desire for you.

At this point in the book, it is essential to remember the soul only wants to evolve. Your soul doesn't care what you are doing in your life. The soul only cares about what you are being while you are doing whatever you are doing. Is this confusing? It is simply a matter of whether you are coming from a place of Love or Fear while you are living your life.

The soul is always providing the perfect conditions for you to do, be and have what is takes to know Who You Really Are. The mind gets to choose from the options your soul provides, and the body acts on that choice. When the body, mind and soul create together in harmony you are co-creating with God.

"There comes a time in the evolution of every soul when the chief concern is no longer the survival of the physical body, but the growth of the spirit; no longer the attainment of worldly success, but realization of Self."
Conversations with God, Book 1, p. 180

"The spirit of you seeks, in the largest sense, that grand moment when you have conscious awareness of its wishes, and join in joyful oneness with them."

Conversations with God, Book 1, p. 174

"Often people attempt to live their lives backwards.
They try to have more things, or more money,
In order to do more of what they want,
So that they will be happier.
The way it actually works is the reverse.
You must first be who you really are,
Then do what you need to do, in order to have what you want."

Shakti Gawain
Remembering Your Soul Purpose
Karen Bishop, p. 14

Chapter 12 Key Points

- Being and Doing

- Your Soul wants to evolve

- There is nothing to do but "Be"

- The act of wanting something pushes it away from you

- You are not your body

- God says it's ok to be happy

New Spirituality Principles

❖ THERE IS NOTHING YOU HAVE TO DO TO BE WHO YOU REALLY ARE

❖ Be-Do-Have-Paradigm

> *"In the true order of things one does not do something in order to be happy – one is happy and, hence, does something. One does not do some things in order to be compassionate, one is compassionate and, hence, acts in a certain way."*
>
> Neale Donald Walsch
> p. 185

Objective

- To create your "Next Highest Vision of Self" by "Becoming" what you want to "Be" without actually having to "Do" anything first.

Preparation and Materials

- Think about the above paragraph from the book.
- Review Chapter 12 about the state of "Being" and "Doing." Think about what you want to choose from the "menu" of "Beingness."
- You will need heavy grade construction paper, scissors, pen pencils, crayons, paints and pictures that represent your next "Highest Vision of Self."

Activity HH

Making "Highest Vision" cards

1. What is your next "Highest Vision for you? What do you want to "Be?" Make some time to be alone each day in your sacred space and think about this question. Record at least twelve different states of "Being" you want to "Be" for this activity. Examples are:

- o I Am a Loving Person
- o I Am a Talented Artist
- o I Am a Wonderful Mother/Father
- o I am Compassionate
- o I Am Kind
- o I Am a Good Friend
- o I Am a Great Public Speaker

2. Take the sheets of construction paper and cut them into twelve equal pieces. Write "My Highest Vision" in large letters on one side of each of your cards. You might want to decorate this a bit.

3. On the opposite side of each card, write down the twelve states of "Being" you have chosen.

4. Next, draw a picture or place something (a stick-figure will do) that represents that state of "Being" to which you aspire on the same side with colored pencils, crayons or paints. Or you can glue a picture on it. Have fun with this!

5. WEEKLY: Place the cards upside down and choose one card each week for twelve weeks. Put the card where you can see it everyday and consciously "Be" that "Highest Vision" of yourself every minute of every day. Act "as if...." even if you do not "think" you are close to "being" this dream.

6. Answer:
   o How did you learn to embody the vision you had for yourself on your cards? What actions did you take?
   o How did you feel about yourself at the end of each week?
   o Did you like each of your new states of "Being?"

> *"When body, mind and soul create together, in harmony and in unity, God is made flesh."*
>
> Neale Donald Walsch
> *Conversations with God, Book 1,* p. 175

Objective

- To further your own evolution of your soul by listening and tuning in to what it wants.

Preparation and Materials

- You will need approximately 30 minutes a day and your notebook.
- Read chapter 12 one more time.

Activity II

1. Go to your sacred space and do the pranic breath work. Every day for approximately thirty minutes, do a meditation, asking your soul what its desire is for you. Listen for your "inner voice" to give you an answer. When you receive the answer to your question, it will be the "highest vision you can think of." In your heart you will know it to be truth.

Remember, your soul is not concerned with doing something with your body. When it knows you are paying attention to what is wants, it will be ecstatic!

2. Write down the answers you receive in your notebook and then think about what they mean. Answer:

   o How can you move in the direction that your soul is asking you to be?
   o Make a list of how you can begin to bring these wishes of your soul into reality.
   o Write at least half dozen "steps" to getting you 'there'

Chapter 12 Questions

Write the answers in your notebook. There is no right or wrong answer. This is for your reflection on what you have learned in the chapter.

You are a human "being." What do you do for a living? (This has nothing to do with making money)

What is your state of "being" when you are doing what you are doing?

What does your soul want?

What can you choose "to be" without "doing" anything?

Further Study:

Read "*The Seat of the Soul*" and "*Heart of the Soul*" both by Gary Zukav to learn more about aligning with your soul.

Questionnaire

 Write the answers in your notebook. These questions are to assist you in recognizing your personal growth after reading the chapter.

What have you learned about yourself after doing these activities?

What feelings did you have during the chapter activities?

Did you change in any way after reading Chapter 12 and doing the activities? If yes, how?

How have you changed in the way you relate to others after reading this chapter?

Conversations with God
– an uncommon dialogue –

Chapter 13

Summary

Trust in the process of life and all good things will come to you. This sounds fairly simple. However, most people do not allow themselves to trust the flow of life and they worry needlessly about everything. This wasted energy, along with such things as fear and hatred can make you very ill.

"Worry is the activity of the mind which does not understand its connection with me.
Hatred is the most severely damaging mental condition. It poisons the body, and its effects are virtually irreversible.
Fear is the opposite of everything you are, and so has an effect of opposition to your mental and physical health. Fear is worry magnified."

Conversations with God, Book 1, p. 188

PEOPLE MAKE THEMSELVES ILL. When you can stop all worry, your health will improve almost immediately because – all illness is created first in the mind. In fact, as God tells the author,

"Nothing occurs in your life – nothing – which is not first a thought."

Conversations with God, Book 1, p.188

For example if you say to yourself, "I always get sick." You most probably will become ill. This and other similar thoughts are like magnets drawing their effect to you. The good news is you can reverse any adverse effects you have created from worry. This requires complete trust in the positive effect of the universe and involves making conscious decisions about everything in your life. Here again is the concept of "New Thinking." Once you make the decision to live your life CONSCIOUSLY, you will live a life free of struggle, moving through life with grace and ease and live for a very long time. In fact, you do not die. Through the sacred mystery of creation and evolution, God designed you to last forever.

"Life is something spiritual. The form may be destroyed, but the spirit remains and is living, for it is the subjective life."

Paracelsus (1493-1541)
(alchemist and physician)
The Lightworker's Way
Doreen Virtue, Ph.D

Chapter 13 Key Points:

- All illness is Self-created

- Worry, hate and fear all attack the body at a cellular level

- Take care of your body

- Life is eternal

- Life is a sacred mystery

- The Soul conceives, the mind creates, the body experiences

- (The circle completes itself)

- You are my body

- God is the Alpha and Omega

- Many mansions

- There is no limit to what you can become

New Spirituality Principles

❖ You are not your body.

❖ Who you are is limitless and without end.

"YOU ARE MY BODY"

Neale Donald Walsch
Conversations with God, Book 1, p. 197

Objectives

▪ To feel God in your body.

▪ To understand that there is no separation from anyone or anything.

Preparation and Materials

Think about the above Neale Donald Walsch quote and the following quote spoken by Jesus: ***"I and the Father are One. You, as my brothers and sisters, my equals, are One with the Heavenly Father. It cannot be otherwise."***

Jeshua
The Personal Christ
Judith Coates, p.38

You have always been one with God. Religionists have made God as this far off being that was so complicated that you never could reach Him/Her. The author of the book shows you the simplicity of it all. You are God and there is nothing that is not God. God is Life. God is the Alpha and the Omega.

Complete the following activity and record your feelings in your notebook. If any questions, come to mind write these down, too. You may choose to record this activity to listen to for a deeper visualization experience.

Activity JJ

Feeling Love, Seeing Love. Knowing How-to

1. Feeling Love
Tomorrow morning, when you wake up, before you get out of bed, feel God's unbounded Love in your body. Can you feel it flowing through your veins and activating every cell in your body? Know that you are that Love of God and you are radiating that Love out from your body. Do you feel it expanding outward? Do you feel the peace that passes all understanding, as Jesus told us about in his teachings?

2. Seeing Love
Continue feeling and radiating that Love out to everything in the room. It may feel silly, but send that Love out to the bed, the chairs, see it in the cat or dog sitting at the end of your bed. See yourself blending, no longer separate from anything. All is the energy of God. Do you believe you are a part of the bed, the chairs, the cat the dog? Remember there is nothing that is not God. Now imagine these things sending Love back to you.

3. Knowing How-to
Feel it until you are so full of Love that you have to go out and joyfully express it to another. When you express that Love of Who You Really Are to others, they will reflect that back to you. Answer:

- How does that feel?
- When you are in that place of Love, does the sun seem to shine brighter?
- Do you notice the songs the birds are singing?
- Are the flowers more beautiful than you ever imaged?

You are experiencing everything for God. You and God are One.

> **"You take rotten care of your body, paying it little attention at all until you suspect something's going wrong with it. You do virtually nothing in the way of preventive maintenance."**
>
> Neale Donald Walsch
> *Conversations with God, Book 1*, p. 190

Objective

- To understand how important it is to your health and spiritual growth to keep ALL body systems in alignment and functioning at the highest level.

Preparation and Materials

Before we begin this exercise, a bit of pertinent background information is important for you to know.

Taking care of your body is essential to your happiness and spiritual growth. You already know how important proper nutrition and exercise is for your physical body. However, it is also important to keep your energy body in perfect working order. This is the energy body or spiritual body that is described in Chapter 3.

It is vital to your health to open and cleanse these chakras to increase your energy flow, which is your life force. If this flow of energy is blocked or slowed down, there will be an imbalance in your body which can lead to illness and dis-ease. The following exercises will take you through a cleansing process of your chakras and auric field.

Go back and look at the diagrams in Chapter 3 that are provided to assist you in visualization of the chakra system and the corresponding auric field.

Activity KK

Cleansing the Energy Bodies

1. Comfort & Relax
Begin by going to your sacred space and be sure you are comfortable.
Breathe in deeply through your nose taking in the prana (golden white light) from your crown all the way down to the bottom of your spine and exhale through your mouth slowly and consciously. Do this two more times and each time imagine that you are releasing any cares or worries and relax as you exhale.

2. Envision:
   o RED
     Now visualize a vortex of energy that is bright red about 3-4 inches in diameter at the base of your spine. This is your root chakra, that grounds you to the physical life. (Look at the chart in Chapter 3 to see what part of the body the chakras correspond to.) See this red vortex of energy spinning clockwise. As it spins, breathe deeply and visualize the golden while light cleansing any discordant energies and see it spinning faster and faster until it is completely cleansed.

- o ORANGE
  Next, move up to the sacral chakra, just below your navel, and see this whirling vortex as bright orange. Bring down the golden white light again and see it cleansing this vortex and watch it spin faster and faster until completely clean. It will now appear as a bright orange top.

- o YELLOW
  Continue upward to the solar plexus area and see this vortex as a bright yellow. Inhale deeply and bring the golden white light down for cleansing until it is rotating faster and faster and glowing brighter and brighter. Visualize it as bright sunlight.

- o GREEN
  Next, move to your heart area where you will see the heart chakra, which is the color of green. Inhale and see the golden white light removing any imperfections on this chakra and continue spinning it faster and faster until it's clean. Its' color will be bright green and pink.

- o BLUE
  Now move to the middle of your throat and visualize a blue vortex spinning clockwise which is your throat chakra. Bring the golden white light over it to cleanse and assist it to spin faster and faster. When it shines bright blue, you will know it is cleansed.

- o INDIGO
  Then move your concentration up to the area between your eyes. This is the third eye chakra, known as the window to your soul, and its color is indigo. Complete the cleansing process again.

- o VIOLET
  Moving to the top of your head, you will find your crown chakra, which is the opening to higher spiritual consciousness. See this vortex spinning as a deep violet color. Bring in the beautiful golden white light and visualize this chakra becoming brighter and brighter and spinning until clean.

3. Practice:
Be sure to do all of these cleansing exercises slowing and consciously. It is important to do this daily if possible; if not at least 2-3 times per week. You will begin to feel more energized and lead a healthier life.

4. Answer:
- o   After doing this activity, do you feel different?
- o   Can you feel an increase in your life force?
- o   How do you think this will improve your life?

"Also – and I hate to suggest this because it sounds so mundane coming, as it were, from God, but – for God's sake, take better care of yourself."

Neale Donald Walsch
Conversations with God, Book 1, p. 190

Objectives

- To connect you with the living energy of the plant kingdom.

- To learn to utilize many essential oils for healing of the body, mind and spirit.

Preparation and Materials

Review the following information

- Purchase essential oils of your choice

- There is a living energy that can help heal the mind, body and spirit. These are the essential oils derived from shrubs, flowers, trees, roots, bushes and seeds. They were used to heal in ancient times, such as in Egypt and Greece, before medicines of our modern times were formulated. You may find as many people do, that these natural substances are much safer for your body and far less expensive to use that the synthetic medications on the market today.

- These oils can be used in cooking, first aid, and cleaning, pet care, aromatherapy, and air purification. The uses of these high vibratory oils have the ability to calm, energize, balance, purify, and rejuvenate.

- For this activity, you will need to experiment with oils. Young Living Essential Oils are of therapeutic grade and one of the best available.

Here are some suggested oils to start with and their uses.

- Peppermint
    - Put in herbal tea to aid in digestion and heartburn
    - Place on bottoms of feet to relieve fever
    - Massage on abdomen to relieve nausea
    - Apply to temples and back of head to relieve headaches
    - Breath freshener
    - Ant repellent

- Lavender
    - Put on palm and pillow to help you sleep
    - One drop on a cut to stop bleeding
    - Place on palms and inhale to alleviate systems of hay fever
    - Kills bacteria on wound
    - Stops itching and rashes

- Lemon
    - Use 1-2 drops to remove gum, oil, grease spots or crayon
    - Use as a disinfectant on hands
    - Clears athletes foot
    - Balances sebaceous glands in oily skin

- Thieves-blend of Clove, Lemon, Cinnamon bark, Eucalyptus radiate, and Rosemary
    - Protects against colds and flu
    - Anti-fungal
    - Helps sinusitis
    - Protective against sore throats and strep infections
    - Balances blood sugar
    - Helps prevent periodontal disease

Have fun experimenting with aromatherapy!

Activity LL

Experiment with the oils you have chosen and record your experience in your notebook. Note how each fragrance or combination affects you:

Feelings
_____
Energy Levels
_____
Mental Sharpness
_____
Stress Levels
_____
Health
_____
?
_____

Chapter 13 Questions

Write the answers in your notebook. There is no right or wrong answer. These questions are for your self reflection on what you learned from the chapter.

Do you know someone who has been under a lot of stress in their life and has had a heart attack?

Has this person changed their stressful environment?

What thoughts have you had that contributed to an illness?

How can you keep yourself healthier in the future?

What does being "eternal" mean to you?

Do you agree with everything you see or hear or read that falls into the paradigm of your understanding, and reject everything which does not?

Can you be more open to things that you cannot see and do not understand?

Are you God? Explain

Further Study:

Begin a practice of yoga to promote flexibility and health and bring all of your chakras into balance.

Questionnaire

 Write the answers in your notebook. These questions are to assist you in recognizing your personal growth after reading the chapter.

What have you learned about yourself after doing these activities?

What feelings did you have during the chapter activities?

Did you change in any way after reading Chapter 13 and doing the activities? If yes, How?

How have you changed in the way you relate to others after reading this chapter?

Conversations with God
– an uncommon dialogue –

Chapter 14

Summary

What is it that you have to learn? Absolutely nothing! You are not here on this planet to learn anything-only experience. And in this chapter, God says have fun in your experiencing. Do what makes you happy, and He/She continues to say that if that fun includes having sex, enjoy it! God tells the author,

"Of course sex is okay. Again, if I didn't want you to play certain games, I wouldn't have given you the toys."
Conversations with God, Book 1, p. 205

You are God Incarnate and you are here to experience it all as many lifetimes as you want. Just be sure you do everything with Love.

What is the most important message in this book? God wants you to know that all life is a conversation with God, and when you listen to that voice inside of you, you will know that you and God are ONE.

"Listen to Me in the Truth of your soul. Listen to Me in the feelings of your heart. Listen to Me in the quiet of your mind.

"Hear Me, everywhere. Whenever you have a question, simply know that I have answered it already. Then open your eyes to your world. My response could be in an article already published. In the sermon already written and about to be delivered. In the movie now being made. In the song just yesterday composed. In the words about to be said by a loved one. In the heart of a new friend about to be made.

"My Truth is in the whisper of the wind, the babble of the brook, the crack of the thunder, the tap of the rain.

"It is the feel of the earth, the fragrance of the lily, the warmth of the sun, the pull of the moon.

"My truth – and your surest help in time of need – is as awesome as the night sky, and as simply, incontrovertibly, trustful as a baby's gurgle.

"It is as loud as a pounding heartbeat – and as quiet as a breath taken in unity with Me."

Conversations with God, Book 1, p. 210

"All the world's a stage,
And all the men and women, merely players;
They have their exits and their entrances,
And one man in his time plays many parts."

Shakespeare
As You Like It

Chapter 14 Key Points

- You have nothing to learn

- Re-incarnation and karma

- Be the cause of your experience

- Sex is joyful and sacred

- Listen to Me

- I Am Always with You

- All Life is a Conversation with God

New Spirituality Principles

❖ Tomorrow's God is not a singular Super Being, but the extraordinary process called Life.

❖ Awareness

❖ Co-Creation Tools:
   – Thought   – Word   – Deed

> *"You are learning nothing here. You have nothing to learn. You have only to remember. That is, re-member Me."*
>
> Neale Donald Walsch
> *Conversations with God, Book 1,* p. 203

Objective

- To understand that there is nowhere you need to go and nothing you need to learn to find God.

- To know deeply that God is always with you.

- To understand that you have been on a grand adventure to nowhere – now here.

Preparation and Materials

- You will need your notebook and some time to reflect and record your feelings.

Activity MM

1. Read the statements below and the questions that follow. Reflect on these and write your feelings in your notebook. Then write about your personal adventure.

- You are God. The way you perceive yourself is the way you perceive God. How do you perceive yourself?
- If you see God outside of you, you will see yourself outside of yourself.
- Do you feel God inside of you?
- Can you feel God flowing through you?

2. Read this and go into your quiet inner space and feeling this story:

God's Love for you is like a parent's love for their child. When you were born to your parents, you felt you were one with them. And as a soul, you were One with God. Then, as you grew as a child, you strayed away from your parents one day, maybe to go play in the sandbox. As a soul, you also strayed from God to go have an adventure. Your parents and God were always there to watch over you. You always came back to the loving arms of your parents, and the soul always came back to the Love of God. Then one day, the child grew up and moved away from his parents and the soul traveled so far on an adventure, he forgot how to get home. You are that soul trying to get home again.

---

3. Take time over the next days and write about the adventure you have been on in your life. Note the ways your soul is helping you get "home" to God.

> *"Yes, there is such a thing as being psychic. You are that. Everyone is that. There is not a person who does not have what you call psychic ability, there are only people who do not use it."*
>
> Neale Donald Walsch
> Conversations with God, Book 1, p. 205

Objective

- To show you that your completely natural "Sixth Sense" can be developed and used to further the evolution of your soul.

According to Dr. Eugene Osty, Director of the Metaphysique International in Paris, humans possess some sensing mechanisms that "go out" and connect on a supernormal level with information that "comes in."

> *Discovering Your Psychic Mind*
> Annette Martin, p. 3

Preparation and Materials

This "Sixth Sense" originates on the right side or feminine side of the brain (explained in the Mysteries of Creation at the front of this book) and contains the subconscious and unconscious mind. You are born with this sense. However, unlike any other sense that you have, you are not encouraged to develop it. When your "Sixth Sense" is working, you are creating an "arc" of energy that reaches over from the right brain to the left brain. Then you will have a feeling, a visual picture, maybe a smell, taste or just a "knowing." The following exercises will help you develop this dormant "Sixth Sense."

You will need a partner for each activity who can work with you. Also, paper to write on, a pen or pencil, several plain white envelopes, a few simple pictures from a magazine or snapshots you have taken.

Activity NN

1. You and your partner could practice pranic breathing and then become completely alert yet in a relaxed state. Your partner will place a picture in one of the envelopes and then put it on a table in front of you. You are to close your eyes and ask the intuitive part of you to show you or tell you what the picture is. A picture of what's in the envelope will pop into your mind immediately and that is the answer. Or you may hear it. You also may have a certain feeling that will give you the answer. Trust in what you "see" and ask your partner to confirm it. Have fun, be relaxed and take turns guessing what is in the envelope.

2. Continue in your relaxed state or return to it by doing your breathing again and now try this exercise. Take a piece of the paper and ask your partner to turn his back and draw a symbol, such as a star, circle, box, etc. on it. Then she will place it upside down on the table in front of you. Ask the intuitive part of you to show you the symbol. When you have a visual, or even hear the answer, tell your partner what it is. Have confidence in yourself. Take turns and have fun with this activity !

"Sex is sacred, too – yes. But joy and sacredness do mix (they are in fact, the same thing), and many of you think they do not."

Neale Donald Walsch
Conversations with God, Book 1, p. 207

Objectives

- To understand what your beliefs are about sex.

- To better comprehend how your beliefs have formed in your life; from where they came.

Preparation and Materials

You will need your notebook and some time over the week to reflect on questions regarding your sexual story.

Activity OO

Writing My Sexual Story

Before you begin to write, think about the following questions and record your answers in your notebook:

1. How did my mother influence my feelings about sex?

2. How did my father influence my feelings about sex?

3. How did other people influence me regarding sex?

4. What are my sexual experiences?

5. Who were the people in those experiences? How do I feel about them now?

6. How do I feel about myself after those experiences?

7. Did I consider sex as a joyous and sacred experience?

8. How did the media influence me regarding my sexual feelings?

9. How do I feel about my body?

10. Am I sensual, sexual and erotic?

- Jot down first thoughts
- Continue taking time and craft sentences for answers to each question above.
- Reflect and sculpt the life picture of you regarding sex
- Write your story. It should be honest and as long as you want to make it. There may be parts that bring up pain, anger and frustration as well as parts that will be full of joy. Let everything come to the surface that needs to, for healing.
- Make sure to tell the pain and tell about your choice to grow past that pain
- Release what no longer serves you, using intention or the ceremony you used in previous chapters. This process can be transformative for your soul.

Chapter 14 Questions

Write the answer in your notebook. There is no right or wrong answer. These questions are for your self reflection on what you have learned from the chapter.

Did you think life was about learning lessons? After reading this chapter, what do you believe the purpose of your life is?

Do you believe sex is joyous and sacred?
Is there a devil?

Do you believe that you have a Karmic Debt to pay?

Do you believe you have always had a "Sixth Sense?"

Have you begun your conversation with God?

What message do you want to send to the universe?

Further Study:

Read more about re-incarnation in the book *Many Lives, Many Masters* by Dr. Brian L. Weiss and *Many Mansions, the Edgar Cayce Story on Reincarnation* by Gina Cerminara

Questionnaire

Write the answers in your notebook. These questions are to assist you in recognizing your personal growth after reading this chapter.

What have you learned about yourself after doing these activities?

What feelings did you have during the chapter activities?

Did you change in any way after reading Chapter 14 and doing the activities?
If yes, How?

How have you changed in the way you relate to others after reading this chapter?

Listening to God

If you listen you can hear God.

You can hear God inside of You.

And if you listen more closely, you realize that it's not an idea or Guidance. It's Energy.

If you listen even more closely, you merge with that energy.

And then you have a choice.

Do I accept this Energy as Myself?

by Nancy Lee Ways
inspirational words of Oneness given to me
and written down after a meditation

God Flows through You

"There is a vitality, a life force, an energy,

a quickening that is translated through you into action;

Because there is only one of you in all time,

this expression is unique. If you block it, it will never exist

through any other medium and it will be lost.

The world will not have it.

It is not your business to determine how good it is,

nor how valuable it compares with other expressions.

It is your business to keep it yours, clearly and directly.

To keep the channel open."

Martha Graham

About the Author

Nancy is a spiritual teacher and ambassador of Light that has dedicated her life to the enlightenment of all sentient beings on the Earth, through the path of the Goddess. Her purpose is to teach everyone, in her own individual way, about the return of the feminine energy and how each and every one of us can reunite the consciousness of the divine creation mysteries and become whole, become One once more.

Nancy with Neale Donald Walsch in September 2006

She has used her feminine intuition and connection to the God-Goddess to complete this Guidebook and hopes that this book, along with the work of Neale Donald Walsch, will be a great resource and bring all who read it to a place of personal empowerment.

Nancy teaching

She accomplishes her sacred work by being a spiritual teacher, author, photographer, and healer in addition to her work with children. Her first important work with children was done through her daughters. One is an Indigo child or spiritual warrior who came to the planet to shake up the system of education and help the world evolve. This knowledge opened Nancy to the "bigger picture" and gave her the desire to work with and teach others about these amazing 21st Century children.

One special teaching opportunity came to Nancy through the School of the New Spirituality, where she worked with a team to set up a curriculum and open an after school program in Atlanta, which included teaching classes and workshops. She also used her marketing skills to develop relationships with the media and set up collaborative ventures with other local spiritual organizations. Then Nancy stepped into a leadership position as Co-Director of SNS Atlanta and worked to permanently establish the learning center in Atlanta.

She has written numerous articles for newspapers and authored "first person" stories for a national spiritual magazine to teach others what she has learned from the "unseen metaphysical world" which Spirit reveals to Nancy in her beautiful orb photography.

She traveled with twelve other women on a pilgrimage to southern France to align with, and embrace her part, in the sacred planetary purpose of the soul of the Magdalene. Afterwards, Nancy traveled Europe and Asia to do spiritual work with people from all over the world, and published articles about spiritual revelations she has received as a result.

Atlanta
September 2008

Oneness

You are my Mother and Father, I am your child of Light!

One night, as I placed my head on my pillow, I feel asleep and had a long deep dream. I dreamed that I was lost and separated from you and could not find you. I looked everywhere for you and longed to be with you again and feel your loving embrace. I traveled everywhere and had many exciting adventures that were filled with joy and much pain. However, my greatest suffering was felt in my separation from you, and I had journeyed so far away from you, I forgot who I was.

After eons of searching for you, this morning, I awoke from the seemingly never ending dream. I felt you everywhere. I felt myself warmly wrapped in your arms, as I lay in my bed. Then I slipped out from under the bed covers you cuddled me in, and as I opened my eyes, I saw you everywhere. As I walked to my window and was greeted by the sun, I saw you shinning down upon me. As I opened the door and felt a warm breeze on my face, I felt you kiss my cheek. I saw your face looking back at me in the orange colored hibiscus flowers growing outside. As I drank my orange juice for breakfast, I took you into me. As I touched the fur of my little dachshund, I was touching you. As I glanced at my husband reading the paper, I saw you looking back at me through his eyes. And, as I hugged my daughter, I embraced you and you embraced me.

I have grown up, dear Mother and Father. I do not need you anymore. I know we were never separated. It was all a dream.

And as I sit at my computer typing, it is God sitting in this chair. I can say with tears of joy and gladness, that I know that I am God and we are ONE.

I re-member . . .

The dialogue begins . . .

I have heard the crying of your heart. I have seen the searching of your soul. I know how deeply you have desired the Truth. In pain have you called out for it, and in joy. Unendingly have you beseeched Me. Show Myself. Explain Myself. Reveal Myself.

I am doing so here, in terms so plain, you cannot misunderstand. In language so simple, you cannot be confused. In vocabulary so common, you cannot get lost in the verbiage.

So go ahead now. Ask Me anything. Anything. I will contrive to bring you the answer. The whole universe will I use to do this. So be on the lookout; this book is far from My only tool. You may ask a question, then put this book down. But watch.

Listen.

The words to the next song you hear. The information in the next article you read. The story line of the next movie you watch. The chance utterance of the next person you meet. Or the whisper of the next river, the next ocean the next breeze that caresses your ear – all these devices are Mine; all these avenues are open to Me. I will speak to you if you will listen. I will come to you if you will invite Me. I will show you then that I have always been there.

Always.

Neale Donald Walsch
Conversations with God
-an uncommon dialogue-

Endnotes

Introductory Sections

Conversations with God Book I
Chapter 1, page 58

Marcus Aurelius
The Light Shall Set You Free
Page 278

Bhagwan Shree Rajineesh
A Cup of Tea

Conversations with God Book I
Chapter 1, page 44

Natural Rhythms
by Lisa Michaels

Conversations with God Book I
Chapter 14, page 207

The Light Shall Set You Free
Page 243, 244

Chapter 1 Endnotes:

Conversations with God Book I
Chapter 1, page 26

Conversations with God Book I
Chapter 1, page 58

Sathya Sai Baba
The Lightworker's Way, page 43

Henry David Thoreau
Remembering Your Soul Purpose, p. xvii

Conversations with God Book I
Chapter 1, page 58

Conversations with God Book I
Chapter 1, page 11

Animal Speak
Ted Andrews

Nature Speak
Ted Andrews

Chapter 2 Endnotes:

Conversations with God Book I
Chapter 2, page 61

Conversations with God Book I
Chapter 2, page 65

The Soul Never Sleeps
Page 35

Conversations with God Book I
Chapter 2, page 61

Conversations with God Book I
Chapter 2, page 60

Chapter 3 Endnotes:

Conversations with God Book I
Chapter 3, page 75

Conversations with God I
Chapter 3, page 83

The Soul Never Sleeps
Page 55

The Seat of the Soul
Page 194

Conversations with God Book I
Chapter 3, page 77

Conversations with God Book I
Chapter 3, page 76

The Light Shall Set You Free
Page 71

Conversations with God Book I
Chapter 3, page 73

Chapter 4 Endnotes:

Conversations with God Book I
Chapter 4, page 92

Conversations with God Book I
Chapter 4, page 93

The Lightworker's Way
Page 79

Conversations with God Book I
Chapter 4, page 91

The Light Shall Set You Free

Conversations with God Book I
Chapter 4, page 92.93

Conversations with God Book I
Chapter 2, page 61

Chapter 5 Endnotes:

Conversations with God Book I
Chapter 5, page 95

Conversations with God Book I
Chapter 5, page 98
Conversations with God Book I
Chapter 5, page 94

Brihadaranyaka Upanishad IV.4.5
Remembering Your Soul Purpose
Page 92

Soul Never Sleeps
Marian Massie
Page 59

Conversations with God Book I
Chapter 5, page 94

Conversations with God Book I
Chapter 5, page 96

Conversations with God Book I
Chapter 5, page 101

Chapter 6 Endnotes:

Conversations with God Book I
Chapter 6, page 103

Paramahansa Yogananda
The Light Shall Set You Free
Page 41

Conversations with God Book I
Chapter 6, page 105

Conversations with God Book I
Chapter 6, page 105

The Light Will Set You Free
Pages 236, 237

The Kybalion
The Light Shall Set You Free
Page 234

The Heart of the Soul
Page 269

Chapter 7 Endnotes:

Conversations with God Book I
Chapter 7, page 114

Conversations with God Book I
Chapter 7, page 115

The Kybalion
Page 38

Conversations with God Book I
Chapter 7, page 113

Conversations with God Book I
Chapter 7, page 115

Chapter 8 Endnotes:

Conversations with God Book I
Chapter 8, page 122

The Light Shall Set You Free
Page 365

Conversations with God Book I
Chapter 8, page 126

Conversations with God Book I
Chapter 8, page 121

Ralph Waldo Emerson
Nature Speak, p. 13

Chapter 9 Endnotes:

Conversations with God Book I
Chapter 9, page 152

Soul Never Sleeps
Page 38

Conversations with God Book I
Chapter 9, page 154

Buddha
The Light Shall Set You Free
Page 213

Conversations with God Book I
Chapter 9, page

Chapter 10 Endnotes:

Conversations with God Book I
Chapter 3, page 83

Conversations with God Book I
Chapter 3, page 83

Paramahansa Yogananda

Shakti Gawain
The Light Shall Set You Free
Page 155

Conversations with God Book I
Chapter 1, page 17

Chapter 11 Endnotes:

Conversations with God Book I
Chapter 11, page 162

Conversations with God Book I
Chapter 11, page 168

Dr. Albert Einstein
The Light Shall Set You Free
Page 302

Conversations with God Book I
Chapter 11, page 164

Hasidic saying
The Light Shall Set You Free
Page 299

A New Earth
page 190

Chapter 12 Endnotes:

Conversations with God Book I
Chapter 12, page 180

Conversations with God Book I
Chapter 12, page 174

Shakti Gawain
Remembering Your Soul Purpose
page 14

Conversations with God Book I
Chapter 12, page 185

Conversations with God Book I
Chapter 12, page 175

Chapter 13 Endnotes:

Conversations with God Book I
Chapter 13, page 188

Paracelsus
The Lightworker's Way
page 89

Conversations with God Book I
Chapter 13, page 197

Jeshua
The Personal Christ
page 38

Conversations with God Book I
Chapter 13, page 190

Conversations with God Book I
Chapter 13, page 190

Chapter 14 Endnotes:

Conversations with God Book I
Chapter 14, page 205

Conversations with God Book I
Chapter 13, page 210

Conversations with God Book I
Chapter 14, page 205

Conversations with God Book I
Chapter 13, page 210

Shakespeare
As You Like It
The Light Shall Set You Free
page 53

Conversations with God Book I
Chapter 14, page 205

Discovering Your Psychic Mind
page 3

Kindly Contact:

SNS, Inc.
After Hours Programs, Retreats, Camps, Trainings, & Materials
for
Youth and their Adult Leaders
Ages 3-103 !

~ School of the New Spirituality ~
Correspondence Office
Post Office Box 622
Tyrone, Georgia 30290
USA
www.SchooloftheNewSpirituality.com

Info@SchooloftheNewSpirituality.com

~ Leadership, Community-Building Kits ~
SNSatlanta@yahoo.com

~ Parent Pathway Team & Eyes Wide Open Store ~
Laurie@SchooloftheNewSpirituality.com

~ SNS Communications, Website & Community Postings ~
Alecia@SchooloftheNewSpirituality.com

~ SNS Dallas & FREE2BU Parent Empowerment Kits ~
Angel@SchooloftheNewSpirituality.com

"Other New Spirituality Principles as shared through Neale's other books"

New Spirituality Principles

Enumerated within the *Conversation with God* ***books***
— many principles are featured in more than one *Conversations with God* ***title —***

The Three Statements of Ultimate Truth are:

1. We are all one.
2. There's enough.
3. There's nothing you have to do.

---

3 Core Concepts of Holistic Living—Living as a Whole Person—Body-Mind-Spirit

Awareness—Honesty—Responsibility used to:

1. Redefine yourself as individuals
2. Redefine yourself as a society
3. Redefine "success"

These replace the 3 P's:
    Productivity
    Popularity
    Possessions

---

5 Fallacies about God

1. God needs something.
2. God can fail to get what God needs.
3. God has separated you from God because you have not given God what God needs.
4. God still needs what God needs so badly that God now requires you, from your separated position, to provide it.
5. God will destroy you if you do not meet God's requirements.

---

5 Fallacies about Life

1. Human beings are separate from each other.
2. There is not enough of what human beings need to be happy.
3. To get the stuff of which there is not enough, human beings must compete with each other.
4. Some human beings are better than other human beings.
5. It is appropriate for human beings to resolve severe differences created by all the other fallacies by killing each other.

Characteristics of *Tomorrow's God*

1. Tomorrow's God does not require anyone to believe in God.

2. Tomorrow's God is without gender, size, shape, color, or any of the characteristics of an individual living being.

3. Tomorrow's God talks with everyone, all the time

4. Tomorrow's God is separate from nothing, but is Everywhere Present, the All In All, the Alpha and the Omega, the Beginning and the End, the Sum Total of Everything that ever was, is now, and ever shall be.

5. Tomorrow's God is not a singular Super Being, but the extraordinary process called Life.

6. Tomorrow's God is ever changing.

7. Tomorrow's God is needless.

8. Tomorrow's God does not ask to be served, but is the Servant of all of Life.

9. Tomorrow's God will be unconditionally loving, nonjudgmental, non-condemning, and non-punishing.

Principles of the New Spirituality (New Revelations)

1. God has never stopped communicating directly with human beings. God has been communicating with and through human beings from the beginning of time. God does so today.

2. Every human being is as special as every other human being who has ever lived, lives now, or ever will live. You are all messengers. Every one of you.

You are carrying a message to life about life every day. Every hour. Every moment.

3. No path to God is more direct than any other path. No religion is the "one true religion," no people are "the chosen people," and no prophet is the "greatest prophet."

4. God needs nothing. God requires nothing in order to be happy. God is happiness itself. Therefore, God requires nothing of anyone or anything in the Universe.

5. God is not a singular Super Being, living somewhere in the Universe or outside of it, having the same emotional needs and subject to the same emotional turmoil as humans. That Which Is God cannot be hurt or damaged in any way, and so, has no need to seek revenge or impose punishment.

6. All things are One Thing. There is only One Thing, and all things are part of the One Thing That Is.

7. There is no such thing as Right and Wrong. There is only What Works and What Does Not Work, depending upon what it is that you seek to be, do, or have.

8. You are not your body. Who You Are is limitless and without end.

9. You cannot die, and you will never be condemned to eternal damnation.

The 3 Basic Life Principles
        1. Functionality
        2. Adaptability
        3. Sustainability

Which replace: Morality - Justice - Ownership

The New Gospel:

"We are all One."

"Ours is not a better way, ours is merely another way."

Be-Do-Have Paradigm

The "Be-Do-Have Paradigm" is a way of looking at life. It is nothing more or less than that. Yet this way of looking at life could change your life—and probably will. Because what is true about this paradigm is that most people have it all backward, and when they finally get it straightened out and start looking at it frontward, everything in their lives shifts 180-degrees. Neale Donald Walsch writes:

Most people (I know I did) started out with the understanding that how life worked was like this: Have-Do-Be. That is, when I HAVE the right stuff, I can DO the right things, and then I will get to BE what I want to be.

When I HAVE good grades I can DO the thing called graduate and I can BE the thing called employable—might be one example. Here's another. When I HAVE enough money I can DO the thing called buy a house and I can BE the thing called secure. Want one more? <u>Here goes</u>: When I HAVE enough time I can DO the thing called take a vacation and I can BE the thing called rested and relaxed.

See how it works? This is how my father, my school, my society told me that it works. Life works this way. The only problem was, I was NOT getting to BE the things I thought I was going to get to be after I had done all that I thought I had to do, and had all the things that I thought I needed to have. Or, if I did get to BE that, I only got to be it for a short period of time. Soon after I got to be Òhappyó or Òsecureó or Òcontented,ó or whatever it was that I thought I was going to get to be, I found myself once again UNhappy, INsecure, and NOT contented ! I didn't seem to know how to Òhold onto the stuff.ó I didn't know how to make the flavor last. So it always seemed as if I did all that I had to do for nothing. It felt like wasted effort, and I began to resent that in my life.

Then I had the *Conversations with God* experience, and everything changed. God told me that I was starting out in the wrong place. What I needed to do was BEGIN where I thought I was going to GO.

All creation starts from a place of BEING, God said, and I have had it in the reverse. The trick in life is not to try to get to be Òhappy,ó or be Òsecure,ó or whatever, but to start out BEING happy, or BEING content, of whatever, and go from there in the living of our daily lives.

But how do you do that if you don't HAVE what you NEED TO HAVE in order to be happy, etc.? That's the question, and it's a fair one. The answer is that coming FROM a state of being, rather than trying to get TO a state of being, practically assures that the Òhavingnessó end of the equation is taken care of.

When you come FROM a state of being, you need to have nothing in order to begin the process. You simply select, quite arbitrarily, a state of being, and then come from that place in everything you think, say, and do. But because you are thinking, saying, and doing only what a person who is being happy, contented, or whatever, thinks, says and does, the things that a happy or contented person winds up HAVING come to you automatically.

Let's try this out and see if it really can work that way. Let's say that what a person wants to BE is the thing called Òsecure.ó If that is the desired experience, what we can do is startOUT from the square on the playing board that says, I AM SECURE. We start out with this idea, and this is the operating idea behind everything we do. We have moved into the BE-DO portion of the paradigm.

When a person does what only a secure person would do, that person almost automatically winds up having what only a secure person would have. Try it out some-time. It's amazing how this works.

The 5 Attitudes of Godliness
1. Joy
2. Love
3. Acceptance
4. Blessing
5. Gratitude

The Prime Value
Life itself is the Prime Value

This replaces the world's definition that the Prime Value is power

---

The Triad Process

1. Nothing in my world is real.
2. The meaning of everything is the meaning I give it.
3. I am who I say I am, and my experience is what I say it is.

5 Steps to Peace

Step 1   Acknowledge that some of your old beliefs about God and about Life are no longer working.

Step 2   Acknowledge that there is something you do not understand about God and about Life, the understanding of which will change everything.

Step 3   Be willing for a new understanding of God and Life to now be brought forth, an understanding that could produce a new way of life on this planet.

Step 4   Be courageous enough to explore and examine this new understanding, and, if it aligns with your inner truth and knowing, to enlarge your belief system to include it.

Step 5   Choose to live your life as a demonstration of your highest and grandest beliefs, rather than as denials of them.

---

7 interchangeable words for God:

Love
Life
Joy
Peace
Freedom
Change
You (Me, Us)

The 5 Levels of Truth-telling

1. Tell the truth to yourself about yourself.
2. Tell the truth to yourself about another.
3. Tell the truth about yourself to another.
4. Tell the truth about another to that other.
5. Tell the truth to everyone about everything.

The Seven Steps to Friendship with God are:

Know God
Trust God
Love God
Embrace God
Use God
Help God
Thank God

Tools of Creation

1. Thought
2. Word
3. Action

The Divine Dichotomy

By moving from an either/or world to a both/and world, I see that both "this" and "that" can be true at the same time, and that allows me to see much more of how things really are in the world around me.

Example: is the rain good or bad? Desert or flood?

The Ten Illusions

1. Need Exists
2. Failure Exists
3. Disunity Exists
4. Insufficiency Exists
5. Requirement Exists
6. Judgment Exists
7. Condemnation Exists
8. Conditionality Exists
9. Superiority Exists
10. Ignorance Exists

These illusions have created humanity's cultural story, from which our present difficulties emerge. The cultural story of humans is that . . .

1. God has an agenda. (Need Exists)

2. The outcome of life is in doubt. (Failure Exists)

3. You are separate from God. (Disunity Exists)

4. There is not enough. (Insufficiency Exists)

5. There is something you have to do. (Requirement Exists)

6. If you do not do it, you will be punished. (Judgment Exists)

7. The punishment is everlasting damnation. (Condemnation Exists)

8. Love is, therefore, conditional. (Conditionality Exists)

9. Knowing and meeting the conditions renders you superior. (Superiority Exists)

10. You do not know that these are illusions. (Ignorance Exists)

The 18 Remembrances from *Home with God, in a Life that Never Ends*

1) Dying is something you do for you.

2) You are the cause of your own death. This is always true, no matter where, or how, you die.

3) You cannot die against your will.

4) No path back Home is better than any other path.

5) Death is never a tragedy. It is always a gift.

6) You and God are one. There is no separation between you.

7) Death does not exist.

8) You can't change Ultimate Reality, but you *can* change your experience of it.

9) It is the desire of All That Is to Know Itself in its own Experience. This is the reason for all of Life.

10) Life is eternal.

11) The timing and the circumstances of death are always perfect.

12) The death of every person always serves the agenda of every other person who is aware of it. *That is why they are aware of it.* Therefore, no death (and no life) is ever "wasted." No one ever dies "in vain."

13) Birth and death are the same thing.

14) You are continually in the act of creation, in life and in death.

15) There is no such thing as the end of evolution.

16) Death is reversible.

17) In death you will be greeted by all of your loved ones—those who have died before you and those who will die after you.

18) Free Choice is the act of pure creation, the signature of God, and your gift, your glory, and your power forever and ever.

School of the New Spirituality
Youth People's Programs
and Programs for Leaders of Youth, ages 3-103 !

The School of the New Spirituality's curricula, materials, and programs promote, empower, and enable love—love of self, family, friends, and community (local to global). Developing a loving peace inside you can create great joy; such inner caring and peace actually shifts the world to a different energy level. A personal 'peace moment' is a fundamental building block to world peace. Self-love leads to a compassion and understanding of our humanity, our commonalities with others, of all living beings, and our ONEness as spiritual beings having an earthly experience.

To contact

School of the New Spirituality, Inc.

Retreats, Camps, Trainings, Interactive Materials and Fun Kits
for
Children and their Leaders

SNS, Inc.
Post Office Box 622
Tyrone, Georgia 30290
USA

To locate additional information about the School of the New Spirituality and Neale Donald Walsch,

Please contact us at:

www.schoolofthenewspirituality.com

For SNS Atlanta, contact

SNSAtlanta@yahoo.com

Index

God (cont.)
  That which you are 75
  Requires nothing 10, 11, 77
  Love in action 77, 78
  Has unconditional love for you 79
  Designed you to last forever 96
  Alpha and Omega 77, 96, 97
  Are One 3, 46, 75, 97, 98, 105
  Love of 77, 98
  Extraordinary process called life 107
  Masculine and feminine 9, 10, 13, 14, 15
  Path to 37, 39, 40
Goddess 17
  Feminine part of 15
  Energy is returning 115
God space, being in spiritual game 19, 53, 54, 55
Gratitude
  Give to God 3, 5, 11, 35,
  High vibration 71, 72

H

Hate
  Attacks the body 96
  Negative thoughts 24, 71, 72, 84
  Low vibration 71, 72
Heaven
  On Earth 38, 45
  Experiencing 38
  Enlightenment 37
  How do we get to 37
Highest vision
  Of self 18, 70, 91
  activity 20, 92, 93

I

I Am
  God 71, 117
  Always with you 106
Illness 95, 96, 99, 103
  Thoughts contribute to 95, 103
  Imbalance can lead to 99
  Self created 96
Illusion
  in old way of thinking 85
  world is an 84
  of insufficiency 83
inner voice, hearing in sacred space 93
Institution, Chapter 4 key points 30

J

Jeshua /Jesus
  You are my brothers and sisters, My equals 97
  Peace that passes understanding 98
Judgment, by someone 46, 50, 54, 77

K

Karma, reincarnation and 106
Killing, is it justified if 73
Knowing
  Sixth sense 109
  Universe will send what you asked for 33, 42

L

Laughter, exercise to reduce stress 50
Law
  God has established 17
  Of vibration 51, 71, 72
  Of rhythm 47, 48, 51
  Cause and effect 46, 54, 55, 56, 58
  Of nature 49
  Universal 18, 47, 51, 55, 56, 72
Living 3, 11, 19, 42, 55, 69, 71, 84, 89, 93, 96, 101
  Energy of essential oils 101
  Without expectations 42
Love
  Unconditional 56, 79
  God's 77, 98, 108
  Do everything with 105
  Radiating 98
  Is the only answer 3, 7, 79
  "in action" 77, 78
  Soul's desire to feel perfect 76
  Highest feeling 17, 75, 76
  True nature 75
  Positive thoughts 71, 84
  Hatred ceases by 70
  Self empowering 31
  Sponsoring thought of 81
  Pink light 100
Lows, law of rhythm 47, 48, 49, 63, 114

M

Masters, set passions aside 38
Medicine 63, 101
  From plants
  Essential oils
Meditation, doing in sacred space 61, 62, 93, 113
Messages
  God's 1, 4, 5, 6, 8
  Learn to send and receive with mind 34
  From Nature Kingdom 8
  From Animal Kingdom 8
Messengers you are all carrying 61
Money 20, 33, 81, 85, 86, 90, 93
  Thoughts of lack 86
  Connection to inflow and outflow 86
  Root thoughts regarding 84
Mother 63, 64, 65, 91, 110, 117
  Influence, regarding sex 110
  Relationship with nature 63

N

Nature
    Quiet place to meditate 31
    Relationship with 63
    Kingdom 63
    spirits 65
Negative feelings
    Low vibration 71
    Throw out all 29, 32
    Anger, envy, fear, hate 71

New Thinking,
    living with consciousness and trust 83, 84, 85, 86, 96

O

Others
    Buying into beliefs of 82
    Based on experience of 10, 12, 81
    Giving power away to 69, 73
    Sending vibrations 72
    Approval from 69
    How spiritual body interacts with 24
    forgiving 14

P

Pain
    Eliminating 45
    Is unreal 46
Parents
    Beliefs based on 10, 11, 12
    Loving arms of 25
    Independence from 56, 57
Passion
    Chapter activity 41
    Drives us to express Who we Are 41
    Path to self-realization 38, 39
    Renouncing 38
Path to God
    Only one true to God 37
    Through the heart 37
Positive thinking, high vibration 71
Portrait, of who you are 73
Poverty, consciousness 83, 84
Prayers, invitation to God to communicate 5
Prosperity 24
    First Chakra 23
    abundance 84
Psychic abilities 22, 108, 122
    In-Sight 22
    Sixth Chakra 23
Punishment, by God 41, 69, 77
Purpose 1, 2, 4, 9, 18, 24, 38, 59, 60, 63, 73, 76, 90, 111, 115, 119, 120, 121
    Of life 60
    Of evolution 61
    Of relationships 59
    Third Chakra 23
    God's for you 1

Q

Quabalah, regarding the Tree of Life 27
Questions, at end of chapters 7, 15, 27, 35, 42, 51, 57, 66, 73, 79, 86, 93, 103, 111

R

Rays xxiii
    golden white light 99, 100
    You are a xxiii
Realization-self, who you are 1
Reiki 27
    Energy 27
    Read more about 27
Re-incarnation, read more about 70, 73, 106, 111
Relationships 22, 59, 60, 63, 66, 67, 115
    Inter-with energy or spiritual body 21, 22
    To help you heal 67
    Bless all 60
    With mother nature 65
    romantic 59
Religion 12, 20, 21, 37, 39, 60, 85, 97
    Root thought regarding 85
    There is no one 39
Renunciation, or passions 38
"right" and "wrong," there is no 12
Root thoughts, not true thought 81, 83, 84, 85

S

Sacred
    Space xxi, 5, 7, 21, 31, 33, 40, 41, 50, 62, 64, 73, 91, 93, 99
    Honoring directions xxii
    Sex 109, 110, 111
Self-Realization 1, 9, 10, 13, 38, 39, 54, 75
    Journey to self 10
    Passion is the path to 39
    Accomplished by experience 10
    Who you really are 1, 3
Sex 24, 85, 105, 106, 109, 110, 111
    Mystery of creation 96
    Second chakra 23
    Joyous and sacred 110, 111
    Experiences 110
Shakespeare, As You Like It 106, 122
Sin, greatest based on experiences of others 10
Soul
    Evoluion of 90
    Third eye window to 23, 100
    Aligning with 93
    Body is instrument of 89
    Desire for perfect love 17, 75, 76
    Feeling is language of 3
Spirituality 3, 11, 19, 30, 39, 46, 54, 60, 61, 70, 77, 83, 90, 97, 107, 115
Sponsoring thought
    Of love or fear 3
    You can change 81

My Own Conversations with God

_____

_____

_____

_____

_____

_____

_____

_____

_____

_____

_____

_____

_____

_____

_____

_____

_____

_____

_____

_____

_____

_____

_____

_____

_____

My Own Conversations with God

My Own Conversations with God

_____

_____

_____

_____

_____

_____

_____

_____

_____

_____

_____

_____

_____

_____

_____

_____

_____

_____

_____

_____

_____

_____

_____

My Own Conversations with God

_____

_____

_____

_____

_____

_____

_____

_____

_____

_____

_____

_____

_____

_____

_____

_____

_____

_____

_____

_____

_____

_____

_____

_____

_____

My Own Conversations with God

_____

_____

_____

_____

_____

_____

_____

_____

_____

_____

_____

_____

_____

_____

_____

_____

_____

_____

_____

_____

_____

_____

_____

_____

_____

_____

_____

My Own Conversations with God

_____

_____

_____

_____

_____

_____

_____

_____

_____

_____

_____

_____

_____

_____

_____

_____

_____

_____

_____

_____

_____

_____

_____

_____

_____

_____

My Own Conversations with God

_____

_____

_____

_____

_____

_____

_____

_____

_____

_____

_____

_____

_____

_____

_____

_____

_____

_____

_____

_____

_____

_____

_____

_____

My Own Conversations with God

My Own Conversations with God

_____

_____

_____

_____

_____

_____

_____

_____

_____

_____

_____

_____

_____

_____

_____

_____

_____

_____

_____

_____

_____

_____

_____

_____

_____

_____

My Own Conversations with God

_____

_____

_____

_____

_____

_____

_____

_____

_____

_____

_____

_____

_____

_____

_____

_____

_____

_____

_____

_____

_____

_____

_____

_____

My Own Conversations with God

_____

_____

_____

_____

_____

_____

_____

_____

_____

_____

_____

_____

_____

_____

_____

_____

_____

_____

_____

_____

_____

_____

_____

My Own Conversations with God

_____

_____

_____

_____

_____

_____

_____

_____

_____

_____

_____

_____

_____

_____

_____

_____

_____

_____

_____

_____

_____

_____

_____

_____

My Own Conversations with God

_____

_____

_____

_____

_____

_____

_____

_____

_____

_____

_____

_____

_____

_____

_____

_____

_____

_____

_____

_____

_____

_____

_____

_____

_____

My Own Conversations with God

_____

_____

_____

_____

_____

_____

_____

_____

_____

_____

_____

_____

_____

_____

_____

_____

_____

_____

_____

_____

_____

_____

My Own Conversations with God

My Own Conversations with God

_____

_____

_____

_____

_____

_____

_____

_____

_____

_____

_____

_____

_____

_____

_____

_____

_____

_____

_____

_____

_____

_____

_____

_____

_____

_____

My Own Conversations with God

My Own Conversations with God

My Own Conversations with God

Printed in the United States
132027LV00001B/21-34/P